OUR BELOVED *Red*

A SON'S MEMOIR ON THE LOSS OF HIS MOTHER

By, Ryan Krohn

Author's Note

To my readers, because I care: in the name of authenticity, and due to the extreme emotional nature of the events that transpired, please note that there is an occasional use of expletives. It was not used gratuitously, or for shock value and it is my sincere hope that you do not take offense. Also, some of the names have been changed to protect the innocent.

Writing this book was a very tough thing to do at times. I want to thank my family, wife, and friends for encouraging me to follow my dreams. Although my mom isn't here with us, she is definitely smiling down on all of us. This book is a celebration of her life. We love you mom. PDLK FOREVER!

Dedication

This book is dedicated to my mother, Patricia Dorene Langs Krohn. She was a saint living on earth. She was the most generous and caring person I ever encountered. Without her love, guidance, and support, I would be nothing.

Introduction
The Day That Changed Everything

"Ryan! Mom's been in an accident down at the light!" My dad was in a panic and yelling as he opened the back door to our house. "It looks really bad."

My heart skipped two beats and a weird tingling sensation went down my spine as I looked at the horror on my dad's face. I have *never* seen this look on his face before. As I tried to digest what he'd said, he was panicking, running around the house and then he picked up the phone.

I felt like I couldn't breathe. "What?" I gasped.

"Mom is laying in your car down at the intersection. There's people all over the place. It's a damn nightmare."

I took about two seconds, collected these thoughts. Is this a dream? I ran through the kitchen and bolted out the backdoor into the yard. Even though it was a cool night, I was sweating like crazy. I had to run down there as fast as possible. No. This can't be happening.

It was about a hundred yards from our house to the intersection. I was an athlete—excelled at the quarterback position, was good at running away from two-hundred-and-fifty-pound lineman—but I had never *ever* run this fast in my life. Halfway there, my heart was pounding hard with every running stride.

As I made my way over the little hill, I saw flashing lights, a crowd of people and cars spread out like wild fire. Sirens blasted in the distance. Ambulances, firefighters and police officers engulfed the intersection. I still couldn't believe this was happening.

I was now thirty feet away. My head felt dizzy and I was nauseous, my pulse raced and my heart palpitated wildly, looking at a whole world of chaos. As I approached the intersection, the look of terror I had seen on my dad's face just a few minutes earlier had now transformed to mine, I am sure. My heart fluttered and skipped a few beats.

I looked and there it was—my shiny, green-metallic Bonneville was completely smashed—but that was the least of my worries.

There was an angel lying in the driver's seat with her head down. Her beautiful red hair was the only thing I could see. The firefighters were using the *Jaws of Life* to open up my car so they could get to my mom.

I looked at the sky. My little perfect world was over in a flash. That day, everything changed.

Chapter One
Red

The color red means many different things to people. Red is hot—it's a strong color that conjures up a range of conflicting emotions from passion to anger and even heartbreak. Red can be good and red can be evil. Red is cupid or the devil.

The expression *seeing red* indicates anger and may stem not only from the stimulus of the color, but from the natural flush of the cheeks from the physical reaction to anger—increased blood pressure, or physical exertion.

Red is power, hence the red power- tie for business people and the red carpet for celebrities and VIPs. Flashing red lights are a warning denoting danger or emergency. Stop signs and lights are red to get the driver's attention and alert them to the dangers of the intersection. In some cultures, red denotes purity, joy and celebration.

To me, the color red means *everything*. For my family, too, it encapsulates many different meanings and connections. Red always brings to mind my mother's trademark red hair. With a slim figure, pretty face and a smile that could light up any room—nobody hesitated to call my mother beautiful. The abundant red curls were a defining characteristic in what made her who she was. When people remember my mom, they remember her passion for the kids at the school in which she worked. They think about the intense love she held for her husband and three children. They think about her positive outlook on life and her passion for it.

Charles Swindoll once stated that life is 10 percent what happens to us and 90 percent how we react to it. My mom lived by this, but in the beginning of my life, I was definitely the kind of person who was sometimes easily frustrated. Now, this is one of my favorite sayings of all time and it rings a bell so true for me. Learning to live life this way can help transform problems into solutions and it can help translate sadness into happiness.

I remember learning a valuable lesson on attitude when I was around eleven. Being a lover of all sports, I played everything you can imagine. I focused on basketball, baseball and football—but among these, basketball was undoubtedly my favorite. I played it all the time and winning the Hillsdale County Free-throw Championship meant everything to me.

The competition was called the Elks Hoop Shoot and kids from all over the area had convened to Hillsdale High School to take part. Participants were placed into age groups arranged in two-year increments from seven to fourteen. My first time out was when I was nine years old and in the third grade. There were around twenty kids in my division that year and I beat them all, making eighteen out of twenty-five shots to take the championship. Pretty good for a third-grader. I had beaten all my friends and even the older ten-year-olds that participated as well. It was nice to win an individual award for something. I was so happy that I was on cloud nine for a couple of weeks after winning.

As competitive as I was—honestly, I didn't know what losing felt like—as a fifth grader in the eleven- to twelve-year-old group, I won the Elks Hoop Shoot for my third straight year. Winning the county tournament gave me the opportunity to participate in the state tourney. In order to prepare, I practiced free throws for hours at a time.

Growing up in Michigan it was cold and snowy for a few months of the year, so it was virtually impossible to practice outside. But sometimes my brother, Damon, and I would put on our snowsuits and shoot outside in our driveway anyway. It didn't work very well and we always came back inside a half hour later with our hands feeling frostbit. Luckily, we had access to the Hillsdale High School basketball gymnasium because my Dad was a teacher there.

I had a month to prepare for the state competition and I was going to do my best. My dad took Damon and me to the gym every Saturday and Sunday. We would line up at our respective baskets and shoot free throws repeatedly. I never got tired of it.

The state competition was twenty-five free throws just like in Hillsdale, and during practice, I consistently made at least twenty out of twenty-five. I had made twenty-two to win the county title and I needed to make at least that many if I wanted a chance to win the state's title. I was even getting to the point where I could make all twenty-five occasionally.

The state tournament took place at a high school in the Detroit area and it consisted of winners from various counties or regions throughout the state. It was a tougher competition because we were all shooting around the same percentage. I was determined to win.

The day arrived. My family and I hopped in our blue Dodge Caravan and began our drive to Detroit. It took almost two hours to get there from Jonesville. I had some serious butterflies going on. It wasn't too often that I got this nervous for anything. After all, at this age I wasn't really into girls that much, I made solid grades—mostly As and Bs—and I was into sports. I was into basketball. I was into winning. This was a way for me to win an individual honor. I played team sports and that was fun, but my teams never won the championship. But in this, I could win the title. I just knew it.

My mom's words that day, like so many other days, remain with me. "Remember, Ryan, stay positive out there and you will do well. If you don't win, it's not the end of the world. Whatever happens, just remember that you tried your best."

I knew that my Mom was right, but at that age, I didn't really get it. I *needed* to win. If I didn't win, it would ruin my day—and most likely my week too.

As we pulled up to the high school, there were cars everywhere. This was a much bigger high school than I was used to. A big crowd was waiting and I wasn't used to that many people watching me. I walked in and saw kids in all different colors, shapes and sizes. When I had walked into a competition in my area, I knew what I was getting myself into and I knew almost everybody that would be shooting that day. But this was different.

After my parents signed me in, I walked into the gym. It was old and it reeked like a dirty gym shoe—a combination of sweat, dust and stale popcorn from the high school game the night before. I took off my old basketball shoes and put on my new ones—Nike Air Jordan's and God help us if I didn't have the new Jordan that came out each season. I inhaled deeply. To me there wasn't anything better than the smell of a new court shoe.

As I tied my shoes, I looked side to side. There were a lot of big kids. Most of them looked older, but I was sure a lot of them were going to be in my division. I was about average size for a fifth grader. However, I felt like I was quite a bit smaller than a lot of these kids, but I reminded myself that regardless of their stature this was a free throw competition, and not a rebounding challenge, so their size wasn't really going to do them any good.

That thought settled me down a little bit. *Just go and do what you do. Shoot free throws. It's just you and the basket.* All I needed to do was pretend that I was shooting in my driveway with my Dad rebounding for me and passing me the ball back.

There were ten kids in my eleven- to twelve-year-old age group. Out of the ten, only two were eleven. I was one of them. We all took some practice shots before we began, then a man with a clipboard announced everyone's names and said where they were from. He sat us down by the half-court line.

For anybody that doesn't know the game of basketball, the Detroit area has produced a ton of great players and most of my competition hailed from the Detroit area, or other larger cities. So it was cool that I was from little ol' Jonesville. There were a couple kids from the Grand Rapids area, and a couple from Lansing, but I was sure that none of them had ever even heard of Jonesville.

When the competition was underway, I was the fourth shooter to go. The first three shot okay as the highest score was only nineteen thus far. Honestly, it had been a while since I had only made nineteen, but anything could have happened. I just had to remain positive like my mom said.

When my name was announced, I got up to the free-throw line and lined myself up with the basket. I looked at the rim and then down at the center point. Often there is a little mark on the center of the free-throw line so shooters know where to stand. I put my right foot down to that mark and I put my left foot about three to four inches back, shoulder width apart.

I took a deep breath and calmly sank five in a row as if it were nothing. "I just gotta keep it up," I said to myself. "I can do this."

The nerves that I'd had before the competition started to fade away. The hoop was my only enemy. Between the shots going in and the sound of the ball dribbling, I could hear people clapping in the distance.

Five more through the hoop and I was ten out of ten. I was off to a real good start. I knew I had to hit at least nine out of the first ten to stay on the pace that I needed. So far so good. I was ahead of the game.

I took a couple deep breaths and hit five more in a row.

"Fifteen out of fifteen," the announcer said. As people started to clap and even take notice from the other side of the gym.

Sixteen, seventeen, eighteen, nineteen. As I released my twentieth shot, I did the same thing I always did—I remembered to bend my knees, keep my arm straight, release with a fluid motion and maintain my form after I released the shot.

Uh oh. This one was different. The ball took a weird little bounce off the back of the rim and started to circle—they call it a "toilet bowl" when the ball spins around the rim. *Go in ball! Come on go in.* The ball spun around once more and it felt like my heart stopped for a minute. Then it spun off the rim and bounced on the floor. *Damn! I had missed one.*

"Wow, that was a close one," the announcer said. "He has hit nineteen out of twenty so far."

I could have lost control and not really cared about the last five shots, but I needed to collect myself and keep a positive mindset. I was already in the lead and I had to keep it that way.

Twenty, twenty-one, twenty-two, twenty-three. I took a deep breath and released the last shot. *Swoosh!* Twenty-four.

"Wow, what a job!" the announcer yelled. "Ryan Krohn from Jonesville with twenty-four out of twenty-five free throws made. That easily puts him in 1st place with six shooters left."

Well that was fun, I had thought to myself. I could breathe a sigh of relief. Missing only one gave me an excellent chance of winning the championship and then going to Washington D.C. for the national competition.

Five more shooters go and the highest anybody got was twenty-two. The last shooter was announced and his name was Ryan as well. He was from Pinckney, Michigan. It is a smaller town close to the Howell and Brighton area. It was about the same size as Jonesville, but it was certainly closer to the Detroit area than we were.

He was a twelve-year-old, a little taller than I was and had short dark hair. He was the only one that could beat me.

He sank ten in a row as if it were nothing. Then fifteen out of fifteen shots and I don't think he had even hit the rim yet.

"Dang, this could get very interesting," a kid next to me said.

Twenty out of twenty. Really? I missed one lousy shot and I might actually lose.

Here we go.

Twenty-one, twenty-two, twenty-three. "What a display of shooting," the announcer said. "He needs one to tie and two to win."

I swear I had stopped breathing. The tension around me was palpable I'm sure.

The other Ryan took a deep breath and looked at the

9

basket. He had a smile on his face. He shot and released. Twenty-four. He had just tied me. I couldn't believe it. My mood changed and I lost my generally happy attitude, becoming more concerned and worried.

Could I possibly lose this? What about the all the hard work practicing for the competition? All those Saturdays and Sundays at the gym with Damon and my Dad just shooting free throws.

Bounce. Bounce. Bounce. The other Ryan dribbled three times. The whole gym was quiet, everybody eagerly awaiting his twenty-fifth and final shot. The shot is up...and it's good!

"A perfect twenty-five!" the announcer yelled as the whole crowd cheers in amazement.

All I could do is just shake my head. I couldn't believe it. I had lost. I had just won second place. How could this be? I thought twenty-four would be good enough to win.

I looked up into the stands at my mom and dad. My mom smiled and mouthed the words, "You did a great job, Ryan. You did your best."

Afterwards, they passed out medals to all ten competitors. The top three places all received trophies. As they announced my name, I tried to put a smile on my face. However, deep down I was hurting and upset—it was all I had cared about for the last month. As nice as it was to get a trophy, I hated to get the silver one. The silver one meant that I got second place. The other Ryan earned the gold one. The one that I wanted. We shook hands and it was time to make our trip back home to Jonesville.

"Good job, Ryan. You did your best," my dad said with a smile. They could tell that I was bummed. I put my sweatpants and sweatshirt back on and we hopped back into our caravan.

"Remember to keep your head up, Ryan," my mom said. "You did really well today."

"I know, Mom. But I didn't come here to get second place. I came to win."

"Well, Ryan, you can't always win everything. Life isn't always fair. And after all, this is just a game. You don't always get your way," my mom said. "You have to stay positive and be happy with your results no matter what. You did such a great job today. Remember, life is all about attitude. It's about how you react to things. If you react to losing in a positive manner, it will show your true character."

Even though, I was still disappointed, my mom's words hit home. Whenever things don't go her way, she doesn't whine and complain about it. She maintains a positive attitude and does the best job that she can.

I learned such a valuable lesson that day. I wanted nothing more than to win first place. It didn't happen. At first, I was sad and upset. I thought I had failed. I learned to look at the positives in what happened and to keep a positive mindset. My mom had reiterated to me the importance of an optimistic attitude, and from that moment on I would keep one. It was just a game after all, and it was a lesson learned. Although I didn't think too much of it at the time, it would speak wonders later on in my life.

Chapter Two
Mom's Life

With all due respect to everyone else in my life, there has never been anyone more influential than my mom— Patricia Dorene Langs Krohn. I can say that with such a big, bright smile on my face. With thick, beautiful red hair, a pretty face and an infectious smile, she was one of the most beautiful people that God ever created.

My mother was born in the same hospital as I was, she was raised in the same village of Jonesville and she went to the same high school. As the daughter of small business owners, R.D. and Dorene Langs, my mother grew up with the small-town way of life. The kind of life where everybody knew everybody—the same kind of life that I had.

My grandparents were hard-working, small-town parents and they instilled great values and morals in my mother from day one. She was raised in the way that many great American families were raised back in the good old days. To them, having great character wasn't defined in words or actions derived out of a fairy tale, for them it was just life—real life. Responsibility and respect were words they lived by. In my opinion, that is something that is lacking in today's society.

Back then, children had the utmost respect for their parents. There was no talking back without consequences and there was no disrespecting their teachers, principals, business leaders or other prominent figures in society. My grandparents had a very positive influence on the person my mother became. These same values and morals would be bestowed onto my sister, Taryn, my brother, Damon and me from my mother and father many years later.

As a kid, I was told how athletic my mom had been. People said she ran faster than all the girls—and most of the boys—and she could throw a softball with the best of them. In elementary school, she could beat most of them in arm wrestling.

Unfortunately, she never got a chance to play sports in high school because Jonesville High School didn't offer any sports for girls. Even by the time she graduated from Jonesville in 1972, they still didn't have them. It wasn't until the very next year that Jonesville High School finally introduced girls' sports.

My mother did participate in cheerleading, though and was actually coached by an English teacher that I would later have. Quite a few teachers that my mother had that would teach me twenty-plus years later.

Mom got along with everybody in her class and she never judged her classmates on looks, ethnic background, or how rich or poor their parents were. She finished high school as the salutatorian next to her best friend, who was the valedictorian. She was a role model for other classmates and for her younger sister, Shari, as well.

Accepted to Michigan State University in East Lansing Michigan, the very same MSU where a lot of her relatives had attended and graduated, my mother lived in the dorms with her best friend, Alicia Lessard. Life couldn't have gotten any better. Except one thing. One thing in her life was missing—my father.

My dad, Steven Michael Krohn had graduated high school from nearby in Litchfield. Litchfield High School was a little smaller than Jonesville and was only a few miles down the road. My dad was the star athlete of

Hillsdale County and every girl in the area was infatuated with him. Ultimately, for reasons I would see later in my lifetime, my dad chose my mom out of all those girls that adored him.

My parents began their relationship during their senior year of high school and they would later get married in March of 1977. According to them, they fell in love almost immediately. It was a tale of true love at first sight. They spent every possible minute together in the summer leading up to college. The only obstacle they faced was going to different colleges in the fall.

My father attended Albion College to play basketball and major in partying—at least that's what we gathered from the stories my Aunt Janis told.

It wasn't a long drive from Michigan State to Albion, just barely over an hour it wasn't hard to travel from one city to the other. However, things were a little different during these times. Especially under the circumstances of where and when they grew up. My parents grew up in a very conservative area in the 60s and early 70s. It was 1972 when they were freshmen in college and people at that age were more respectful of rules and stipulations.

Nowadays, eighteen-year-olds will do whatever they want and not tell their parents about it, but back then, even though they didn't live under the same roof as their parents, a lot of kids would still seek permission to hang out. In order for my dad to visit my mom, he needed to borrow a car to drive up there. My dad's parents loved my mom and vice versa, but borrowing a car would become a hassle.

My parents were like Romeo and Juliet in the way that being together was their only true happiness and they wanted to be together all the time. Obviously, this couldn't happen if they went to separate schools. So, after much deliberation, my mom and dad decided they wanted to go to the same University. This would bring them the utmost happiness they so rightfully deserved. They had wondered where they could both go that would suit their needs. The answer was Western Michigan University—the place my Grandma and Grandpa Krohn met and where I would eventually attend too.

Located in Kalamazoo, Michigan, it was the perfect place for them to study together. It's not too big or too small. My parents both wanted to be teachers and they felt WMU would prepare them to make this dream happen. According to my dad, he needed somebody to watch over him as well since his grades had suffered a little at Albion. He needed to focus if he was going to be a teacher and my mom always kept him on track.

After they had completed the necessary classes as education majors, they participated in the mandatory student-teaching program. They were now on the path to graduating. My mom graduated in 1976 and my dad followed in 1977.

It was now time to enter the real world. Mom landed a teaching job at Climax Scotts, which was a small town close to Kalamazoo and the perfect size for her. My dad ended up getting a teaching job at Harper Creek Middle School, which, like Climax Scotts, was a smaller area and close to Kalamazoo.

They both kept their respective teaching jobs for a couple of years, but something was missing—they wanted to be around their family more. They were on the verge on getting ready to have kids and they wanted to be closer to where they grew up. So, with a little bit of help from my uncle, my dad was able to obtain a teaching job at Hillsdale High School. This new job enabled them to move back to Jonesville where they felt they belonged.

My mom was able to land a job in Hillsdale at a family employment agency. She would counsel those in need of a job and a better life. They couldn't have been happier.

My parents bought a house on the outskirts of Jonesville. Life was perfect. The year was 1980. It was now time to think about having kids.

Chapter Three
Growing Pains

I wasn't always a hard-partying kid. Matter of fact, I was completely the opposite. Even as a youngster, I was afraid to get into trouble. I was quite the rule-stickler according to my mother's journal. She stated there that I was afraid to get into trouble and when faced with the chance of being scolded by adults, I would get nervous and sometimes sick to my stomach. She couldn't have been more spot-on.

When I was a little kid in elementary school, I thrived on getting my teachers' approval. Very curious and inquisitive, I asked questions all the time to both my mom and my teachers. I wasn't a teacher's pet kind of student because I was always one of the most popular kids in class. On the other hand, I knew how to talk to teachers to get help without coming off as a suck-up.

Recess was my favorite time—going outside and feeling free of worry, even if only for fifteen minutes, we made the best of it. We played basketball, football, baseball, softball, kickball and dodge ball. With the athletic genes I got from both my parents, I excelled at sports, even as a young kid. I was one of the few fifth graders that got invited to participate with the big sixth graders. They all called me by my last name and asked me to play because I was good enough to keep up with them. Even though I was smaller than most of them, I could hold my own on whatever sport that we decided to play that day. Basketball was usually our game of choice. Normally, we would start a game and it would last all day. There were three recesses, two short ones and a longer one at lunchtime. Then the next morning we would pick teams again.

I never liked to get into mischief. At Williams Elementary school, we had two ladies that patrolled during recess to monitor the students on the playground. They gave out pink slips to kids that got in trouble for whatever reason. The pink slip consisted of the date, time and nature of the offense and it had to be signed by your parents that night. If you didn't bring the pink slip back the next day, you couldn't go out for recess. You would have to stay in the classroom while all the other kids got to play and at this point in our lives, this was a big deal. I had some friends that got one almost every week. One of my buddies in fifth grade set the record by receiving a whopping twenty-seven pink slips over the course of the year. The ladies that ruled the playground were very strict.

I went all the way through my elementary career never receiving a single pink slip. Even though many of my friends got them, I still managed to stay out of trouble. I'm revealing these memories not to brag about how well I behaved, but as a testament to how my parents raised us.

Part of it was my natural character, but my parents always instilled high morals and values in us. They told us to treat others the way we would want to be treated. I was never rude or disrespectful. If I disagreed with a friend or a teacher, I never created a scene or caused a fuss. Sure, I made mistakes like everybody else, but the key was to minimize them and then learn from them.

Taryn, Damon and I always got along with everybody, including our teachers and the administrators that roamed the hallways of our schools.

I never got into much trouble in junior high or high

school either. In my entire high school career, I only got one Saturday school detention. Jonesville High School rarely had an after school detention so detentions were held on Saturdays. My girlfriend had gotten in a fight in one of her classes. Some girl had called her a few names and then a shouting match began. The other girl struck my girlfriend in the face before being grabbed by the teacher. They were both sent down to the principal's office.

It was very uncommon for my girlfriend to act in such a way. The other girl was a troublemaker and notorious for starting fights with people, so my girlfriend didn't end up getting in trouble, but the other girl received detention.

When I found out about it at lunchtime, I consoled my girlfriend. I had said, "That girl is bitch," out loud and one of the principals just happened to be walking by that very moment.

"Excuse me, Mr. Krohn?" he scoffed. "What did you say?"

"I...I didn't say anything," I replied.

"Come and see me when the bell rings," he demanded.

"Okay," I said.

Great. I was about to get in trouble. With the football playoffs looming, the last thing I needed to worry about was a damn Saturday school.

I kissed my girlfriend goodbye and walked into the principal's office. I was really nervous. Some of my friends were amused with my little transgression. They knew I never got in trouble. After I sat down, I pleaded my case with the principal. I told him it's not even that big of a deal and that I was sorry I said it, that I was just reacting to the girl who hit my girlfriend in the face.

Considering I'd never been in trouble, you would

have thought he could let me off the hook. It's not as if I punched someone or called somebody a name to their face. It really shouldn't have been a big deal.

The principal must have been on a power trip that day because he gave me my first Saturday school detention ever. I had to report to room 221 at eight a.m. for four hours. My perfect record of no detention just went out the window. I was sure that I would end up sitting next to the girl that started this whole mess in the first place. I thought for sure the principal would give me the same Saturday school as her. Thankfully, she ended up having a different Saturday than I did.

Chapter Four
Game Night

I have so many great memories of high school—hanging out with friends, going to movies, the mall and bonfires in the summertime. The dances were always a blast. Prom was an event that I will cherish forever. I couldn't dance but I was good at making as ass out of myself. Being the class-clown type people had come to expect it out of me. Taking trips with my family and best friends will always be some my favorite memories of high school.

Without doubt, though, some of my best memories involve sports and when it comes down to remembering details, I've always had an uncanny ability to remember sporting events the best. I played football, basketball and baseball at Jonesville High School—but basketball was definitely still my favorite.

The Jonesville basketball team was like an extended family for me. It was like that for all of us. There were complications at times and obstacles to overcome, but for the most part we were like brothers. As my junior year had come to end, we finished with a 21-3 record. We won the districts but lost in the regional championship game. It hurt like hell to lose, but we knew we would be back for more next year.

In my senior year of basketball, by the time we had gotten close to the end of the season, we'd only had one loss. This particular loss fell to the hands of the Quincy Orioles. Our first match-up with them took place without one of our best players in the contest. Kyle was hurt for the first go-round and we still almost beat them.

For the next match-up, we had the league's reigning MVP back and this spelled big trouble for the Orioles. Quincy would be in for a rude awakening this time. To make things even more epic for us, it was homecoming. We were the best team in the league. They had lost a few games and we were determined to beat them down this time. We had concluded there was no way we would lose to an inferior team, especially on our homecoming. We were ready for game day. I just needed to get a good-night's sleep and dream of a big victory.

I woke up nervous the following morning to a special feeling in the air. It was only six thirty a.m. and I already had butterflies. As I walked up the stairs to take a shower, I noticed every creek in the stairs. I jumped in the shower and as the hot water hit my skin, I thought about the plays we were going to run. I dried off and proceeded to get dressed in a shirt and tie, because that's how we rolled on game day.

After I was done getting ready, I walked into the kitchen. My mom gave me some eggs and toast that she had just made for everybody.

"Some breakfast to start off your day." She passed me the plate.

"Thanks, Mom." I smiled.

It was hard for me to eat, but I swallowed it all anyway. As I drove off to school, my stomach started to feel a little better. I walked in to school and I saw students dressed in orange and black from head to toe. They were already yelling my name and giving me high-fives.

It was hard to concentrate in first period and we had a test in American Government. *Awesome*. Go figure we would have a test on game day. Luckily, I could write almost anything in that class and still get an A. The test went so slow as I stared at the clock for about five minutes straight. It was as if my heart beat slower with every passing second. You could have heard a pin drop in that room. I certainly could hear the second hand each and every time.

Second and third period flowed by smoothly. We were now into fourth period Seminar class and I was starting to get drowsy. My teacher's words were going in one ear and out the other. I was dozing off, but I couldn't quite fall asleep.

Lunch was right around the corner and I couldn't wait to stuff my face. It was Friday so that meant we were going to have french toast sticks. Usually I would get double the amount and snarf it down like there was no tomorrow. But, the feeling of nervousness and excitement still fills me with every swallow of my lunch. The pit of my stomach begins to churn. My savior for the afternoon comes in a little twenty ounce green bottle—I'm talking about Mountain Dew and this is basically my daily medicine.

It was now one o'clock in the afternoon and we were getting ready for the last period of the day. The caffeine was now coursing its way through my veins. My hands were trembling a little bit and I had sweaty palms.

The pop doesn't help, although I probably wouldn't be relaxing anyway. Sitting in Algebra II class, I was tapping my foot almost uncontrollably. I couldn't pay attention to linear equations and functions. *Are you kidding me?* I'm sorry. It's just wasn't possible. All I could think about was our opponent and how we were going to defeat them. The whole school was counting on us to retain the Big 8 Championship. My heart fluttered and skipped a beat as every second passed by. *Seriously, come on clock. Hurry up!* We still had ten minutes to go.

Just after the bell finally rang, students started yelling in the halls, "Beat Quincy, baby!" That's all I could hear. I walked into the parking lot and a few teachers wished me luck. As I started my Chevy Lumina, DMX blared from the speakers.

Two of my best friends were meeting me at my house before the game. We didn't have to be there until six o'clock as the Junior Varsity game was before ours.

It was now three thirty and my friends, John and Jake, were sitting with me in my living room watching TV. Jake was on the computer blasting music and John and I were watching ESPN. We were talking about the game a little bit, but we were also talking about the dance and stuff afterwards. It wasn't that we weren't fully focused, but we needed to talk about something else to calm our nerves.

My family got home from their respective school and workdays. They wished us good luck, knowing the importance of this game. I told them goodbye and said I would see them around midnight when the dance was over.

I was feeling really pumped up, but I was starting to get nervous again, too. We drove the short mile and a half from my house to the gym. The junior varsity game had started and we gathered in the crowd with the rest of the guys. There was already a significant crowd at the JV game. I could feel the excitement in the air as I looked over to the visitor's side. I glanced at our enemy for the night and I spotted my arch nemesis. He was joking around with his teammates, but I was fully focused on the game at this point. I was already visualizing the tip-off and the first quarter. I stared at him with my headphones on, blasting DMX.

By the end of the third quarter of the JV game, it was

time to get dressed in our uniforms. Our Jonesville side stood up, clapping and cheering, as we walked into the locker room. I had a nervous anticipation as I put on my orange Jonesville jersey, but I was so pumped up and focused that it would not consume me.

After everyone was dressed and ready to go, we stretched out a bit and listened to Coach talk about some of the plays. The JV game was now over and we could hear the crowd ready to get into a frenzy. The song "He Got Game" started to blast from the stereo system. We ran out for our pre-game warm-up and the crowd went nuts. They knew what was at stake just as much as we did. We were currently first in the league and the other team was in second place. If we won, it would put us even further into first place and almost guarantee the league title.

I was so pumped with excitement during warm-up that with my small but athletic, five-foot-ten, hundred-and-fifty-pound frame, I was effortlessly making layups over the rim. The clock now said five minutes until game time. We ran into the locker room for the final game plan.

Coach encouraged us to run the plays as planned and play tenacious defense. We started yelling and hollering. There was really only one thing on my mind and that was *revenge!* These guys got lucky last time because one of our best players was out, but this time, it would be different.

It was finally game time baby. We lined up and the national anthem was played. My name was called and I shook the other coach's hand. I spotted one of my friends in the crowd so I ran over to him, pointed and proceeded to give him a chest bump. The other four starters followed suit and did the same. We gathered as a team, in a circle, one last time. The crowd was yelling and shouting so loud I could barely hear anyone.

"Let's send these Orioles back to Quincy where they belong," a teammate shouted. A few cuss words ensued as we readied for tip-off.

As we got set for jump ball, I was tense but relaxed in sort of an unusual way. I could see it in the eyes of the players on the other team—they knew they were in for a very long night. The ball was tipped to me and the game was underway. I immediately took three dribbles, spun around and passed the ball to our center. He took one dribble and turned around, laying the ball off the glass. The game was 2-0.

We needed to set the tone early and to play aggressive on defense. We were known for making people turn the ball over. Quincy came at us. I was looking at the waist of my nemesis and he dribbled back and forth. He passed the ball to a forward on the wing. Almost simultaneously, my teammate sprinted in the lane and stole the ball. We were running the other way. I got a step on my defender as the ball was passed to me. There was nothing but the rim and me now. I laid the ball off the glass and it was 4-0 just like that. It wasn't even a minute and we were already making plays.

Then they came down and set up a play. The ball was passed around a few times and then a shot went up—no good. We rebounded the ball and went the other way. Now it was time for our offense to produce. I called a play as directed from Coach. Then I passed the ball to my wingman, cut through the middle of the paint and sprinted to the opposite side of the ball. Right after I cut through, the center ran down to the opposite wingman and set a pick on his man. The wingman ran up to the elbow and caught the ball. He took a jump shot and swished it.

We traded a few baskets, but kept the momentum. We were up 16-8 with a couple minutes left in the first quarter. Then Quincy called a timeout. At this point, it would be huge to come up with a big play. I could see it in my teammates' eyes; almost smell the sweat and desperation on the air. We wanted to put this game away early. With the crowd in a frenzy, we wanted to be winning in a blowout by halftime.

So we came out and set up a play. The ball got passed around like a hot potato and I was wide open on the right wing behind the three-point line. I received the pass and immediately fired toward the cylinder. *Swoosh!* We were up 19-8. The crowd stomped the ground in unison and cheered at the top of their lungs. "Go Comets!" We scored a couple more baskets while they only managed a free throw. That made it 23-9 to end the quarter. We were dominating all facets of the game and they knew they had been hit with a huge uppercut.

"This is homecoming baby," a teammate yelled. "We've never lost on this court and it's not happening today."

We continued to bombard them with tenacious defense and an overpowering offense. We were clicking on all cylinders. Three starters, including myself, were already scoring in double figures. I have eleven points at halftime and we were up 44-24. *Blowout city!* It was only halftime, but so far we had accomplished what we'd set out to do. We were pumped and giving each other high-fives.

Coach Dunn came into the locker room and congratulated us on a great first half. He told us to keep up the pace. "You never know what could happen so don't stop playing hard."

It felt good to have a big lead at halftime, now it was time to put the finishing touches on Quincy. The truth was we had sealed their fate by the end of the first quarter.

When a superior team brings their top level of intensity and aggression, along with an efficient offense, they are extremely tough to stop—and that was us that day.

As the third quarter began, we didn't let up. We hit a barrage of three pointers catapulting us to over a thirty-point lead halfway through the third quarter. It was time for the starters to take a seat and let the reserves play. We probably could have beaten them by fifty points.

The whole Jonesville crowd stood up and applauded our effort. They appreciated hard work and defense and they weren't afraid to show it. That was one of the best feelings ever. Although I love to play, sometimes it's just as fun to watch your buddies play. I had a few close friends that only played in the fourth quarter when we were winning and it was nice to see them get in on the action. We went from being cheered to becoming their biggest cheerleaders. We yelled loudly after one of our teammates made a basket.

As I sat there basking in the glow, I realized my time as a Jonesville basketball player was soon coming to an end. We had a few more games, but this one was special because it was homecoming—an agonizing defeat against this team was simply not an option. The buzzer sounded and we won the game 72-40. A huge, lopsided victory over the second-place team.

After we got out of the showers, our parents and friends were waiting for us. Both of my parents greeted me with a smile and a hug. They told me that I did a good job and that they were both proud of me. A few of my buddies that didn't play basketball were also there and congratulated me as well. It was now time to go to the dance. The dances were fun, but for people like me, the game was what really mattered. Most of all, it was the camaraderie we all shared with each other. The cohesiveness of our team was top-notch and it was fun to share the victory with such a great community of people. For the most part, the whole town came to our games. Whether for a basketball game or a different sport, our little farm-town community supported us to the fullest. They loved to watch their boys play basketball.

Everybody knew everybody in our small town, which made for some pros and cons growing up. It seemed as if everyone knew your business and thought they could give advice even when you barely knew them. However, the pros definitely outweighed the cons and I will never forget the togetherness our team shared with our parents and the community. I get a tingling sensation just thinking about it.

Chapter Five
College

Once upon a time, I was happy without a care in the world. My biggest problem stemmed from contemplating what beer I was going to drink on the weekend, which house party I was going to attend or what girl I was going to try and talk to. Ah...the life of a college student—especially one that attends Western Michigan University, or as we called it, *Waste-ern* Michigan.

My typical weekday consisted of getting up at about ten thirty in the morning, going to a couple classes, playing basketball at the Rec Center, hitting the books for about an hour and then falling asleep to Conan O'Brien between one and one thirty a.m. This was what I did, every Sunday through Wednesday night.

Waking up Thursday morning always produced a special feeling in the air. Most of us didn't have classes on Friday so as soon as we were done on Thursday, it was *on like Donkey Kong*—time for a three-day party. There was excitement around and all of the frowns of frustration and stress turned upside down as music blared from every other house on the street. It gave me the feeling that we were already at a party or club. I didn't know whether to break dance or look for some glow sticks to show off my moves.

I lived with three guys, Danny, Greg and Travis. Greg was the elder statesmen in our household. He was twenty-three and we called him *Grandpa*. He was cool and laidback so he didn't mind the nickname.

Travis was my cousin and just a year younger than I was. He was a lot like me in the sense that he didn't really view college as the most important thing in his life and he was trying to figure out exactly what he wanted to pursue. Majoring in biochemistry, he wanted to be a chiropractor like me, but he had his reservations as well, because he too realized that it was going to be harder than initially anticipated. He cracked us up because he rarely ever went to class, but he was good at taking tests though. He could show up and pass a test without even trying very hard.

Danny was from the eastern side of the state, Walled Lake, and was a junior just like me. He was an education major and wanted to be a teacher. Danny and I had been friends for three years. We had met in a communications class our freshmen year and the rest is history. We shared a lot of common interests in sports, movies, politics, beer, hanging out, partying and women. He was my partner in crime. Well, no crime actually took place, but there were plenty of shenanigans. We studied hard during the week—wrote papers, hit up the library and behaved like gentlemen. But on the weekends, just like most WMU students, it was time to rock-out. We all lived for the weekends.

"What kind of beer do you want tonight, Krohn?" Danny asked, full of enthusiasm.

"Anything but Natural Light, dude. That stuff tastes like piss." We called it Natty Light and while I had drank it in the past, I decided that I would almost rather drink my own urine than that stuff again.

"Well, hell, it's usually one of the lights, man. Just pick one."

Being a broke college student, we always wanted to get the best bang for our buck. Aside from Natty Light, I'm not that picky when it comes to the fine assortment of light beers—Bud, Miller, Coors and Busch. "Screw it, dude. Let's go with Busch Light. It is usually the cheapest. You can get a thirty pack for twelve bucks at Drake's Party Store. Corey is going to get it for us again."

Corey was one of my former roommates. He was a bit too wild for my taste so I could only handle living with him for one year. It was my sophomore year, but even though we had moved on to different living arrangements, we still were good friends and hung out on the weekends from time to time.

Since we were only twenty and Corey was twenty-one, we couldn't legally buy alcohol, but he could. If it wasn't for the ramifications of getting caught, I would have risked getting a fake ID off some willing friend. All one needs to do is walk into the Drake Party Store, look on the *Wall of Shame* and see the mugs of random imbeciles who didn't have their way with the store clerks. The thought of seeing my mug plastered on that wall was enough to make me wait until I was twenty-one. Besides, it wasn't much of a problem to find somebody to buy for us.

Once, we even paid a homeless guy to buy for us. We felt like assholes, but when a college student needs his booze, he needs his booze dammit! The guy appreciated it and I'm sure used the few extra dollars to buy a much-needed pack of smokes or a forty-ounce of King Cobra.

As a junior at Western Michigan, I still had a few months until I was twenty-one and I was salivating at the opportunity to finally be able to get into the bars, but for now, getting *shit-canned* at random parties would suffice.

It was eight p.m. and Corey finally showed up with a thirty pack of Busch Light. Time to get it popping. It was the weekend and we were serious about our partying, we all commenced to "double-fisting" while Danny and I got ready to go out.

By the time Danny had showered, changed four times and spent twenty minutes on his hair, the thirty pack could easily be gone, before we even got to the party. He was notorious for taking longer than most girls do to get ready. Sometimes I called him Mr. Rogers because he changes his clothes so much.

"All right, Sally. Don't forget to use both conditioner and shampoo." I sarcastically chastised him and he smiled back."

"Whatever, bro. You're almost as bad as me," Danny shouted back.

He was right. I was known for taking long showers, especially in the wintertime, but I never changed more than once. Once I thought about what I was going to wear, I would throw it on and that was that. I jumped in the shower with my beer in hand and gulped it down as if I'd been stranded in Death Valley for a week without water. I was out in seven minutes and proceeded to get dressed and add my illustrious spiking gel to my hair. Now I'm ready to rock and roll.

It was only fifty-three degrees out—a nice, crisp Michigan autumn evening. Actually, that wasn't terrible considering it was late October. Usually by this time of the year, it was really cold already.

"You want a shot of *Jager*?" Corey shouted from the kitchen. Jagermeister, more commonly known as Jager, tastes like black licorice and is very smooth. Definitely a popular shot for college students and you don't even need a chaser with it. Unless of course, you're a lightweight, which I wasn't.

"Yeah, buddy, pour me one." I walked into the kitchen looking like a million bucks, if I did say so myself. Corey gave me a nod of approval.

Finally, Danny came out with his gel lying down on his head. "Should I go with laidback-Danny or cool-hip-Danny?" he asked. He spiked his hair kind of like mine while asking the questions.

"Spike it, man," I said.

Danny spiked his hair and took a shot with us. This would be my second shot in less than five minutes. Combine that with my double-fisting of the two Busch lights and I was already four drinks deep in less than a half hour. My buzz had set in and I now had a permanent smile on my face.

As we walked outside, I smelled the fresh air and a mixture of what seemed like barley and hops. We got into Corey's Jeep. Good thing he's only had a couple drinks because there's no way in hell I should drive at this point.

We backed down the driveway and spun off down the street. Danny tried to tell me something from the passenger seat, but I couldn't hear what he was saying because the music was so loud.

"Turn down the music for a second. I can't hear a word that you're saying."

"I said, are you gonna try and talk to Erica tonight, Krohn?"

"I don't know. I guess If I see her I will," I said sheepishly.

Erica was a girl in my chemistry class who I was absolutely infatuated with. She had golden-tan skin, blonde curly hair and a smile to die for—definitely a sight to see. She had a different aura about her, different from any other girl that I had met before.

There were tons of girls at Western Michigan and most of them were from bigger cities. But with Jonesville's population of approximately twenty-five hundred, it wasn't hard to be larger than my hometown. A lot of girls that went to Western Michigan hailed from the Metro-Detroit area. In fact, many of the students seemed to come from the more affluent suburbs surrounding Detroit. Not all the areas are wealthy, but they are much better off than where I come from.

Erica was from the richest of them all. She was from Bloomfield Hills. The same Bloomfield hills where a lot of professional athletes and musicians lived—not to mention CEOs, doctors, lawyers and anybody else that was fortunate enough to be a millionaire.

To say that Erica had a swagger was an understatement. She was always dressed nice and had a designer bag in her hand. Even on lab days, which were every Friday, she was dressed to impress. On those days, she wasn't dressed like a beauty queen, but she just knew how to dress sexy no matter what she was wearing. She was well put together and I was highly attracted to her.

"I want to talk to her," I told Danny, "but it really depends on how many douche-bags will be surrounding her."

Considering we were going to a frat party, there would be a lot of them. We all made fun of the frat boys. Why would you want to pay for friends? Considering there are about twenty-seven thousand students at WMU, one shouldn't have a problem making friends.

"Yes, watch out for the frat boys," Danny said.

Corey laughed. "No shit. When you see a *Beamer* or a *Benz*, you know you found a frat boy."

Even though she came from money, Erica seemed to be down to earth. I got a chance to talk to her every Friday morning during lab. There were around thirty students in that class, divided into six groups of five. My group included her and three other girls. Do I know how to pick them or what?

We rolled down to *frat neighborhood* and it wasn't hard to tell we were getting close to the party. We drove by the house and there was nowhere to park. Benzes and Beamers flooded the driveway along with a couple Audis and a maroon Cadillac convertible.

"We're gonna have to park down the hill," I said. "Hopefully we can find a spot at the bottom."

"Yeah it's about a half-mile walk," Danny confirmed.

There were seriously hundreds of cars lined up and down the streets. Everybody and their brother was going to be there. It was the place to be. Even though these parties were always crawling with frat boys, there would undoubtedly be a ton of girls there too—with frat boys, came sorority girls. Sorority girls were essentially cut from the same cloth as fraternity boys, and like their male counterparts, they drove nice cars and wore expensive clothes.

Normally we wouldn't even consider going to a frat house. One of the main reasons I disliked going to frat parties was because they were very particular on whom they'd invite. They wouldn't just let anybody come. We got an invite because Danny had an old high-school friend that happened to be in this particular fraternity.

My whole goal for the night was to find Erica and talk with her as much as I could. She had told me earlier in the week that she was going to be there. She was actually not in a sorority, but a lot of her friends from high school were.

Chapter Six
Party

"We'll just walk in like we own the place," I said. "Let's just act like one of them."

"You guys have your hair spiked." Corey laughed. "You already do fit in."

"That may be true," I said. "However, we didn't come here in a thirty-five-thousand-dollar car."

We walked up to the door and I felt confident. I didn't want to walk into the room exuding arrogance and close-mindedness, but I did want to walk in with confidence. Half the people in the party would already be so drunk they wouldn't know it if the president walked in and we would use their drunkenness to our advantage.

It has been my experience over the years that girls hate cockiness. However, insecurity is something that they hate even worse. They want you to be tender inside while being confident and masculine on the outside. I tried to maintain that perfect blend. I was the sensitive, nice guy, but I always had a certain aura of confidence about me. Picking up a girl, or just simply talking to her, is directly related to self-confidence and it shouldn't matter what your profession is or if you have money. Whether you are a doctor, lawyer, janitor, or pizza delivery driver should be irrelevant.

I wasn't a rich dude. I came from a middle-class upbringing. We had an average house in an average neighborhood, in a blue-collar farm town. I was raised not to judge someone by how they looked.

I opened the door and I had a smile on my face. We walked right in. I wasn't always this extroverted, but when it was time for Ryan Krohn to turn it on—I could turn it on with the best of them.

For us, it was first things first. Locate the kegs. This *was* a frat party after all and not your typical keg party. There would be several kegs of Oberon here. Oberon is a seasonal, wheat ale and is the most popular beer among Western students. It is a Bell's classic and is brewed right in Kalamazoo and nearby Comstock. Oberon tastes so good that people have even compared it to the sweet nectar of the Gods.

The place was completely packed by ten thirty and it would fill up more in the next couple of hours. I had noticed a few girls in the kitchen area talking to some guys. Every one of them looked like they could pose for Playboy. I wondered why most sorority girls had to be so hot.

"Where the hell is Kevin at?" Danny asked with a grim look on his face. "He's not answering any of my texts. He's got to be here somewhere though."

"He's probably downstairs doing a keg stand or something," Corey said.

I always thought we partied a lot, but this kid could drink and party with the best of them. He had probably been drinking since noon. Actually, there was even a chance that Kevin washed his Lucky Charms down that morning with vodka instead of milk. There was a huge difference between him and us. Danny and I had solid grades, GPAs higher than a 3.0. Kevin didn't care—he had less than a 1.0 and didn't seem to give a shit either way. He always said he would start trying one of these days. Not that it really mattered for some of these frat boys though. They could skate by doing the bare minimum and then get jobs back home working for their father's company. Danny and I had to work hard for everything, but we were better off in the long run for it.

After we made our way through the crowd, I asked somebody where the keg was and he managed to point downstairs. As I walked downstairs, I didn't really see anybody I knew. No Kevin. No Erica—who knew where she was, but considering she hung out with sorority girls, she'd be there at some point.

Typically, at these sorts of parties if you wanted a cup, you'd have to pay around five dollars to somebody that lived at the house. At least that is usually how much it is to get one at a house party.

"How much are the cups?" Danny asked.

"I don't know, let me ask somebody."

There was a crowd of people around one of the kegs. Most of them were frat boys, you could always tell, they just had a different look about them. I was often perceived as being somewhat *metro-sexual*—but these guys all took the cake. They generally had dark hair with blond-tip highlights and their skin looked as though they just came back from a month-long stay in Mexico. Maybe they did. Their clothes consisted of Armani Exchange, Ferrari and Polo. It wasn't even the clothes they wore, it had more to do with the way they carried themselves—with arrogance, as if they thought they were better than everyone else.

They didn't accept all different types of people in their parties. The only other time I had been to a frat party before that night, I saw them kick out a group of girls because they said they were fat and ugly. I was appalled by their behavior. Not that all frat boys are like that, but in my experience the majority of them I had encountered were.

When we had a party at our house, it was come one,

come all. You could be dressed like Kurt Cobain, a stockbroker, or look like a homeless guy straight off the streets. It didn't matter. We welcomed everybody and encouraged everybody to have a great time.

I noticed one of the frat boys had a big stack of red cups. He was probably about six foot four and wearing a purple polo with the collar popped. It wasn't hard to spot him.

"All right, boys, time to get a cup," I said. "Let's see how much these bad boys are." I walked up to the dude and asked him.

He bumps his buddy standing next to him then says, "How many cups do you need tonight?"

I pointed at Corey and Danny. "That would be three cups, dude."

He fiddled with the whiskers on his chin and gave his buddy a big grin. "Okay, cool that'll be thirty bucks, brother."

At the very moment this guy's words came out, Corey got a look of madness on his face. It was crazy to see how fast his face could go from dumbfounded to furious. I looked at Danny and received his smirk with one of my own.

"Ten bucks a piece?" I was rolling with laughter. "I thought you were going to say fifteen bucks total."

"Oh yeah?" replied Mr. Cool. "What the hell did you think this was? A party in the student ghetto?"

"Well, okay," replied Danny with a laugh. "Maybe we'll just go somewhere else for the night."

"You know Kevin Porter, asshole?" Corey chimed in. I'd been standing five feet away from him, but I could smell the potent venom being spewed from his mouth. His fists clenched up as if he was ready to throw-down.

"Kevin Porter?" the frat boy asked. He had a weird

look on his face. "You mean the Kevin Porter that lives here?

"Yeah, he's one of my boys from high school," Danny answered."

"Oh, okay," he replied. "Yeah Kevin is here somewhere. I didn't know that you guys were friends with him."

"Yeah," Danny responded. "I called him a couple nights ago and told him we were coming to the party."

"Well, in that case, it's only five bucks a piece for you fine gentleman. Kevin is a frat brother and if he's your boy then you're cool with me."

He handed us each a cup and I happily accepted. Corey wasn't too pleased, but that didn't stop him from taking his cup. He still had that *fuck-you* scowl on his face, but Mr. Cool didn't really seem scared though. I guess I wouldn't have been either if I'd had about two hundred friends at my house.

"Thanks, man," I said then turned to Danny and Corey. "All right, guys, let's go find Kevin."

Let's just pound some beers and get drunk," Corey said.

"What about finding Erika, boss?" Danny asked. I thought that is the main reason you wanted to come. She will be here right?"

"Yeah, she should be. At least, she told me she would be coming."

We walked downstairs to the basement area. They had a lot of room down there. It wasn't like a typical student party in the ghetto that consisted of a couple hundred students trying to pack into a small nine-hundred-square-foot basement. We had a lot of room to move around. The basement was about five times the size of a normal house. In one of the corners, they had a beer-pong table with people playing and about twenty people watching the action. There was a sweet dance floor, which in itself was bigger than our whole living room. I was sure the floor was nice and shiny at one point, but now it was dirty from all the shoes that had stepped on it.

There was a DJ in the corner of the dance floor and he had a killer set up—strobe lights, a fog machine and speakers the size of an average man—all laid on a platform where the DJ stood. This wasn't just some guy that they hired off the street, apparently it was the DJ that spun at Wayside. Considering Wayside was the biggest bar in Kalamazoo, it had to have cost a pretty penny to get him to leave there for a night. There were people all over the dance floor as *Biggie's* "Hypnotize" blasted from the speakers.

Because I was good at recognizing faces, I saw a lot of people that I knew. Not in the sense that I had once engaged in a conversation with them, but I knew their faces. I can see a face one time and remember it forever.

There was a group of sorority girls standing next to the dance floor, about five of them and all of them were gorgeous. We could tell they were sorority girls because of their green bags inscribed in pink letters with their sorority on them.

"I don't see Erika," I said to Danny. "You heard from Kevin yet?"

"No. That rat bastard isn't answering his phone. I don't know where the hell he's at."

"I'm telling you, his crazy ass got drunk as hell and he's passed out somewhere," Corey said.

"Yeah, but he lives here, Corey. He's got to be at this house somewhere," I said as I gulped down the rest of my cup.

"This is what we should do, boys." I said. "Let's refill

our cups and go talk to those sorority girls. You guys wanted to talk to some girls, so let's do it. Let's hurry and get some more beer before some frat boy jackasses swoop in and spit some game."

"Sounds good to me," Danny said.

We went back upstairs and it was even louder than before. "Keg stand!" The guy pumping the keg yelled loud and proud.

Oh, buddy, this ought to be fun. For those of you who never experienced college or have been living under a rock, a keg stand is an American tradition at a college party. It is when two friends suspend you by your ankles over the keg and you guzzle as much beer as quickly as you can. As the blood rushes to your head, you guzzle and guzzle until you can't drink anymore. Usually, if someone could get to thirty seconds, it was amazing. This particular chap got turned upside down and his face flushed as red as a fire engine within seconds. He made it to twenty before he tapped out. He must have felt everything was copacetic, as he raised his arms in the air and his buddies cheered wildly for him.

After we refilled our Oberon, we went back downstairs. Still no sign of anybody that we knew. The goal was to talk to these sorority girls no matter what. And much to our pleasure, nobody was around them. It was time to go for it.

"All right, boys," I said presumptuously, it's time to go in for the kill."

"You're like a lion preying on a gazelle," Corey said undaunted.

Sorority girls tend to be circuitous, duplicitous and conniving in their aspirations. It seemed to be in their nature. Because of this, I felt armed with even more confidence than usual. Part of it was the challenge, but another part of me felt untroubled because I didn't think they would even acknowledge me. When you have nothing to lose, you don't have much to worry about.

"Hey how are doing?" I said to a tall girl with dark curly hair.

"Uh, hi," she said reluctantly. "Do I know you?"

"Well, my name is Ryan, I have a psychology class with you."

This statement was ballsy as it would certainly make or break me. I didn't know any of these girls. Nonetheless, I had taken a lot of psychology courses and I knew these courses were flooded with sorority chicks. In my mind, there was a decent chance she was a psychology major or minor. If she was, I was *in like Flynn*.

"Oh really? Which one?" she asked.

If she were a psychology major, she would have definitely taken Psychology 101. "Psychology 101," I said in my most confident tone of voice.

"Well yeah. I did that class last year. When did you take it?" she asked.

"Last year," I responded. "I thought I recognized you." Don't be weirded-out, but I'm just really good at recognizing faces."

"Yeah, that's cool," she said. "Our classes are so big, I don't know anybody other than my sorority sisters. My name is Jessica by the way."

I couldn't help but laugh. She probably thought I was laughing at what she'd said. Little did she know, I just pulled this out of my ass and it had worked to perfection.

I turned to Danny and Corey and Corey was shaking his head in amazement. "These are my buddies, Danny and Corey," I said to her.

"Nice to meet you," she said.

She proceeded to introduce us to her sisters. It was as

easy as that. By this time I was feeling no pain and after a couple more trips to the keg, we were all feeling pretty good.

"Do you know what time it is?" Danny asked me.

"What's that, son?" I answered.

"Time to hit the dance floor, playboy," he said with a huge smile on his face.

I thought for a second. "Okay, I'm drunk enough. Looks like the girls are pretty drunk too. Time to hit the floor."

It was after midnight and still no sign of Erika, or Kevin for that matter. The four sorority sisters and us were dancing. I was dancing with Jessica. I had to admit, thus far in the night, my preconceived notion of sorority girls had been proved wrong. That wouldn't last very long though.

Just when I thought nothing could go wrong, there she was. Out of the corner of my eye, Erika had been spotted. The blond curly hair. The crystal blue eyes. She was looking right at me. Her whole entourage was looking at me.

"Do you know that girl?" Jessica asked.

"Yeah it's my friend, Erika. I had a few classes with her when I was a biochemistry major."

"Yeah, I know her too," she said.

"Oh really?" I asked.

We continued to dance. Little did Jessica know I was completely enamored with Erika—the moment I saw her, my body language changed. My dancing had resembled a *Snoop Dogg* video before I saw Erika and deviated to a 1950s sock hop within seconds. I didn't want Erika to see me grinding on anybody. It's not as if we were boyfriend and girlfriend, we weren't even dating, but damn I really liked her. She was genuinely interested in me too, but I thought I might have just blown it.

"Our two groups don't get along," Jessica confided. "Let's just put it at that. Matter of fact, they are basically our rivals and to say we don't get along would actually be an understatement."

Oh shit. Go figure. The group of girls I befriended are Erika's worst enemies.

"Let me go talk to her," I announced.

I had a healthy buzz going on, but at least I wasn't in a drunken stupor. Maybe I could talk my way out of this.

"Hey, Erika. What's up?"

Nothing. Not even a glance in my direction. She turned her head in disgust so I turned her around and looked her in the eye.

"Are these the people that you associate yourself with?" she inquired.

"What do you mean?"

"Those girls are the biggest bunch of bitches that go to this school," she roared. "Why are you dancing with them?"

"I was just hanging out. We decided to dance and there they were," I lied.

"Are you serious now, Ryan? I have been watching you grind that slut for the last five minutes."

"Slut?" I asked pathetically.

"I know that girl. She has hooked up with more frat boys than anybody I've ever met in my life."

"Well, I haven't seen one frat boy talk to her tonight. Let alone hit on her."

"That's because we're at a Sigma Phi party," she snapped. "These guys are rivals with the Sigma Eps house. They hate each other. Who let them in here? They are just here to stir up trouble."

I hollered right back at her. "You know I don't know

any of this frat-boy-sorority-girl bullshit, I couldn't care less. The only reason I was talking to her is because you weren't here."

"Whatever, Ryan. Maybe you aren't the person I thought you were."

"All because I was dancing with her? That didn't mean anything."

"Whatever, I'm pissed. This is bullshit. I'm done talking with you tonight, see you later."

As she walked off with her friends, I was perplexed by what just happened. I just gazed in astonishment as my night of fun was over. My buzz was dead and I was ready to go home.

"What the hell happened, dude?" Danny asked.

"Erika saw me grinding on Jessica, I guess. It's not like I wanted that to happen."

"Yeah, man, that sucks. If she only knew you were looking so forward to just hanging out with her."

"Yeah whatever. It's all good. It is what it is," I said. "Let's bounce."

We went home and passed out in our respective beds.

The next day was Sunday. I called my mom and talked to her for about fifteen minutes. I typically talked to her around three or four times a week. It was more than a lot of my friends talked to their moms any given week. We had so many great conversations on the phone. While most guys call a buddy when they have a problem, I called my mom. She gave the best advice. Not only was she my mother and number one person in my life, she was like my counselor and best friend.

I told her what had happened the night before. I sincerely liked Erika and wanted to get to know her better. She'd caught my eye from day one. I was instantly attracted to her. Because of what had transpired the night before, I told my mom that I might have blown that opportunity.

My mom's advice was always what I needed to hear. She said to give Erika a call and say I'm sorry. Even though Erika had overreacted to the situation, a girl always needs to hear I'm sorry first. Mom told me to explain to Erika what had happened and that all I had really wanted was to hang out with her.

"It's out of your hands now," she said. "If she realizes that she made a mistake and still wants to see you, she will come to her senses. Just tell her that you care for her and you want to hang out, just the two of you. Ask her for another chance. Don't lose your temper and get defensive. If she has already made up her mind and won't give it a chance, well that's the way it goes. There are plenty of girls at Western that would love to hang out with you." My mom was exactly right, like always. She eased my mind and made me feel comfortable about the situation.

I have never been the *player* type. Even though I liked to flirt and talk with different girls, I was always the one-woman type of guy. Being as charismatic as I was, I knew I was the one that needed to strike up that conversation at the party. I just wanted my boys to have a good time. I wasn't trying to go home with anybody that night, unless it was Erika. Meanwhile, trying to do too much cost me a possible relationship with her. I never did hang out with her again. She didn't answer my call that night. I'd left her a message but never heard a response. I saw her months later at a bar and she had a boyfriend. Obviously, things didn't happen for a reason. You live and you learn. My mom taught me that

Chapter Seven
Our Beloved Red

I'm breathing as if I just ran a marathon and my lungs feel as if they are going to collapse with every passing breath of air. I'm sweating so profusely it looks like I just jumped out of our swimming pool. I'm dizzy and feel like I just got off a fair ride.

"Where the hell is everyone at?" I wondered.

"Where was Damon? Taryn? Where was my Dad? I just saw him two minutes ago. Well I think it was two minutes. Not sure. I could have been two hours for all I knew at the time. No, it was indeed two minutes. My dad was on the phone calling my aunt and uncle.

The accident happened on the corner of our street, Walnut Street, and highway U.S. 12. It happened to be one of the busiest intersections in our little village of Jonesville. On the corner of that intersection was the Dairy Treat. This was probably the busiest place in all of Jonesville in the evenings. It was a place for families to go, for baseball teams and their coaches, for boys to take their girlfriends. A place where the elderly hung out and where troublemakers went to check out girls.

The Dairy Treat had the best food and ice cream in the whole area. They had every kind of ice cream you could ever want, and it was the best place to grab a burger and fries. They had a burger called the Double Jay. It consisted of two burger patties, lettuce, tomato and that sauce. *What was that sauce?* It was actually Thousand Island dressing. I always thought there had to be something more, but there wasn't. For some reason that burger with that dressing, tasted like God himself had come down and made it. The grill was fired up and you could smell these tasty burgers being cooked from outside the shop.

"What the hell? Where is everyone?" I ask loudly.

There were about thirty people currently at the Dairy Treat, hanging out, eating or waiting in line. Some of the faces I recognized, some I didn't. However, there was one thing in common—that look of terror. Mouths were wide open and eyes were bulging out as if a flying saucer had just landed in downtown Jonesville. I could sense the clear and utter shock in every one of them.

I turned around and it felt like my body was rotating in slow motion. I looked at my car that my mom was driving, although I could hardly bare to look. The front end of the car was smashed like a pancake and the driver's side was smashed in as well. I could see my mom in the driver's seat, but her head was kind of looking downward at her feet. All I could see was my mom's beautiful red hair shining in the sun.

"Who the hell did this?" How the hell did this happen? I yelled out with an unwavering cry.

There were a ton of police at the spot, but I saw one that I knew. This guy was a friend of the family and my mom thought he was a solid guy as well.

"How did this happen? Who did this?" I questioned him.

He had that same look in his face. Of course, police men are always supposed to remain calm, but even this guy looked unsettled.

"That semi-truck T-boned your mom, Ryan," he said with a look of panic.

"Holy shit! She's going to be okay though, right?"

50

"Uh, Ryan...well, at this point we don't know.

"What? She's gotta be okay. She's just gotta be all right."

"Where is the guy that hit my mom?" I asked George.

"Over there talking to Tom, Ryan."

As he pointed over to the guy, things started to go into slow motion again. Was he going to point at the Devil? Who else could have done such a thing? Even if this was an accident on his part, how could this happen?

I started to walk over to the guy. My feet trembled with every step I took. I got nervous as I approached him. He was a heavyset guy with long scraggily, blond hair tucked behind a trucker hat. He looked like your typical semi-truck driver. As I made my way closer, I didn't know how I would first react. Part of me wanted to break down and cry and part of me wanted to slug him in the face. I envisioned myself being Mike Tyson for a split second and knocking him out cold with one blow to the head.

I knew deep down inside this isn't the way I would react. Everybody that knows me knows this. It's just not in my nature to explode on someone physically. Even when I had a reason.

"How could you have done this?" I asked.

He turned around and looked at me.

I looked at him the same way I would look at a monster. "You must not have been paying attention!" I yelled.

"I couldn't...I couldn't see. The sun was in my eyes...It was an accident," he said with a tremble in his voice.

I couldn't even answer back. I couldn't get into this right now. My emotions were running higher than they had ever been in my life. There is no way I could deal with this. In the grand scheme of things, he didn't matter. All

51

that mattered was my mom. I had to go back over and see if I could fight my way through all the firefighters.

"Ryan, you can't go over there right now," George yelled. "The firefighters have the Jaws of Life out because they are trying to get your mom out of the car.

"What the hell am I supposed to do, George? Sit here and do nothing?" I spouted with anger.

"You have to let these people do their job, Ryan." He seemed to force the words out of his mouth. "Everybody is trying to help."

Time slows down when something like this happens. Psychiatrists, scientists and all doctors alike will tell you something changes in your brain chemistry during a time of panic. It was an experience that changed me forever. As much as I tried to forget what it felt like, I never will.

I walked back up to the Dairy Treat parking lot. At this point, the whole area was flooded with tons of people. I'm sure a lot of them were looking at me. I was in such a zone that I didn't really notice anybody down there. Jesus Christ himself could have come down from the heavens and I probably wouldn't have noticed. I just stood there looking at my mom. The firefighters were still trying to get her out with the Jaws of Life.

A few more minutes passed. They are still trying to get our angel out of my car.

What in the hell is taking so long? The ambulance is here. She should be in there by now and en route to Hillsdale Hospital.

Finally, Damon walked up with a few of his friends. I could tell by his body language that Damon didn't know it was Mom. I walked over to him, each stride closing the gap between us. We met at the end of the road, about ten feet from the Dairy Treat.

"Damon! Mom just got hit by a fucking semi." My

language was none too appropriate around all these parents and children, but at that moment, it didn't matter to me—this was a matter of life and death.

"Holy shit. It's Mom!" he shouted.

"Yes. She was t-boned by that semi-truck." I pointed in the direction of the truck. "They're getting her out right now. We gotta get a ride to the hospital."

"Where is Dad at?" Damon asked.

Almost simultaneously, we looked up and my dad appeared. He was with our next-door neighbor, Matt Molinaro. Matt was a close friend to my mom and dad and to us too.

"Boys, you're going to go with Matt to Hillsdale Hospital. I'm going to stay here until they get her in the ambulance. Then I'm going to drive over," my dad informed us.

Damon and I hopped into Matt's car and we sped off. There was still a ton of people at the intersection. An anxious audience just stood and waited as everything unfolded. It's only about five miles to the hospital in Hillsdale, but the complete silence between Matt, Damon and me made it feel like a lifetime and the blink of an eye all at once. Matt was always a very talkative guy, but I'm sure he just didn't know what to say to us at that moment.

"God, she better be okay." Damon shook his head. He was in shock, too.

"She's gotta be okay, right Matt?" I asked.

"I'm sure she will be okay, guys. She probably just has a concussion and maybe a broken leg or something," he did his best to reassure us with a calm voice.

Matt was speeding, practically flying down the road. But it was an emergency—and hell, there wasn't a police car in sight—they were all in Jonesville at our intersection. We zipped through Hillsdale and finally pulled up to the front of the hospital. Damon and I jumped out and dashed into the hospital while Matt parked his car.

As soon as we entered the sliding glass doors, the receptionist was staring at us. It felt really weird. I had been to that emergency a couple dozen times in my life and it was always packed, but I swear there was nobody in the waiting room. It was like a ghost town. The receptionist motioned us over to the front desk. Damon and I looked at her and we both sighed. When we were in front of her, she told us that Dr. Smith wanted to talk to us right away.

We took about five steps around the corner of her office and opened the door to the hallway. Dr. Smith was actually our family doctor, we've known him for years, and he happened to be in the emergency room that evening. I noticed him sweating a little bit, almost in a panic. He wiped the sweat off his brow and took off his glasses.

"Hey, guys," he said to Damon and me. "Your Mom isn't coming here. She is being *life-flighted* as we speak to Ann Arbor. She is going to the University of Michigan Hospital."

"What? Why in the hell is she going there?" I demanded.

"Your mom is unconscious. We can't give her adequate treatment here. They are the best." Matt walked in and Dr. Smith told him the same thing he just told us.

"What the fuck!" I said to Damon, "This is not good.

"I swear if something is really wrong with her, I'll lose it, man," Damon uttered under his breath.

We got back into Matt's car and sped off again. It still felt like I was in a dream. It didn't feel like reality. At least it was only five miles back to the intersection. I had driven between Hillsdale and Jonesville over a thousand times in my life. We didn't have everything in Jonesville that we needed and making a trip to Hillsdale was inevitable at times. It was typically a very nice and easy drive, but not this time—this was a drive from hell. The anticipation of getting back home and not knowing what to expect was eating my insides.

We rolled back into Jonesville only to drive up to a whole line of cars. It was actually backed up because of the accident and there must have been twenty cars in front of us. *Screw this! We needed to get around these vehicles.* Fortunately, Matt had some balls and drove around the cars. We got about fifty feet from the intersection only to be immediately stopped by a police officer. He was directing traffic. He walked up to us and told us that we needed to wait our turn. There were plenty of cars ahead of us so we shouldn't be swerving around anybody.

"These are the Krohn boys," Matt said. "The woman in the accident is their mother. How is she doing?"

"I don't know how she is doing, sir. I'm just here doing my job," the police officer said. His businesslike approach was an affront to us and to the emotional turmoil we were experiencing. *Thanks a lot buddy, thanks for the help.*

Damon and I couldn't wait. We jumped out of Matt's car and ran up to the intersection. At this point, I saw our lives flash before my eyes again. The only thing remotely comforting about the situation was that I finally saw more family members. Taryn was there with my dad. My Aunt Shari and Uncle Larry were there as well.

Apparently, my Uncle Larry went up to Rosalie's to get Taryn. Rosalie's was a restaurant just a mile up the road from our intersection. My sister went to Western Michigan University as well. Like me, she was done for the semester. She waited tables at Rosalie's during the summer to earn money.

Damon and I embraced Taryn. She was crying and it made me tear it up a little more.

"What's going to happen?" she said.

"I don't know," I replied.

Taryn, Damon, my dad and I jumped back into Matt's car. He would take us to Ann Arbor to see my mom. My Aunt Shari and Uncle Larry would meet us there. It was now time to face our biggest fear. Our mom's life was in danger and we were lost and without a clue.

Chapter Eight
University of Michigan Hospital

As we arrived close to the University of Michigan Hospital, we'd been in the car for about an hour. That's all it takes to get to Ann Arbor from Jonesville, but for some reason, it felt like five minutes—as if time had almost stopped from the moment I had run down to the crash site.

As we passed by signs that said University of Michigan Hospital, my hands trembled even more as I was faced with a realization that this could actually be real. We stopped and got out.

"Let's go, guys," my dad said.

The temperature was in the high seventies, but a very chilly sensation overtook my body. As soon as we walked in the doors of the hospital, we were met by somebody we knew. It was Alicia Lessard. She had been my mom's best friend since they were little kids. Typically, she greeted us with a big warm smile on her face. However, this time was different. She had a very scared look on her face—she was just as concerned and frantic as we were.

"Oh my, Steve. Come here." She gave my dad a big hug while tears were streaming down her face. "I got here as fast as I could," she said.

"Let's go see her," dad said, letting go of Alicia. The wetness of her tears left a darkened stain on my dad's shoulder where she had been leaning.

Two doctors and a nurse motioned us over to the desk. "We have a conference room for you guys," said one of the doctors.

A conference room for what?

The room was about the size of my bedroom. There were ten chairs arranged in a circle. We all took a seat— my dad, Taryn, Damon, Matt, Alicia and me.

"The doctors will be with you in a few minutes," the nurse told us with a concerned look on her face and then she left.

"How are you guys holding up?" Alicia asked.

"Not good. Not good at all," Taryn said, with a frown.

"We just want to know what the heck is going on," Damon said.

I could hear them talking, but it was as if I wasn't there. My body was, but my brain wasn't. It was floating off into space.

We only waited there for a few minutes, but it felt like an eternity. Then the door opened and it was as if I could feel every creak in the door as it moved inwards. My heart started to pound and sweat poured off me. My skin was clammy and I felt like I had just run a marathon.

It was my Aunt Shari and Uncle Larry. Thank God it wasn't the doctors! My mind could rest for a few more moments. Well, at least for a second. My Aunt Shari was very emotional and she could barely talk. She was crying uncontrollably. We were all feeling the same fear of the unknown.

Alicia stood up and walked over to her. My father did the same. Aunt Shari grabbed both of them. Her hands were wrapped around them and her fingers were visibly trembling.

"What do we know?" my Uncle Larry asked.

"We don't really know anything yet," Matt stated. "The doctors are supposed to be here any minute now to tell us what is going on."

A million thoughts raced through my head. I wanted the doctors to end the speculation, yet I was dreading them coming in. I was so afraid of what they were going to say. I didn't know what I would do if it was something serious. Matt had me convinced that it was just going to be a few broken bones and a concussion. The idea that it could be something worse was mind-blowing to me.

We sat there in that room. Some of us crying and some of us anxious and ready to hear the verdict.

"Where are we at right now?" my dad asked my Uncle Larry. "Are we in Kalamazoo?"

"We're in Ann Arbor Steve. We're at U of M Hospital."

My dad was panicking a bit and he seemed to be confused. I understood because I was feeling the exact same way. It was from the shock and unless you've been through it, you don't really know how to explain it. It seemed that each one of us was suffering from this acute stress reaction in our own ways.

Suddenly, the door opened. My body froze as the doctor walked in. It was as if I had just seen a ghost. I'm sure my face was as white as snow on a cold snowy Michigan day. The doctor looked to be in his fifties, average looking with a medium build and average height. He had glasses and thick gray hair. He took a chair, biting his nail while scanning over his audience.

I can't imagine what that felt like—having to tell a group of people potential life-altering news. The closest I could come to fathoming it was when I was a Junior Varsity basketball coach and I had to tell a few kids they didn't make the team. That was tough to do, but it obviously pales in comparison.

"Patricia has been in our intensive unit for a little over an hour now," he announced. "I am the leader of the traumatic brain injury team."

Traumatic brain injury? That doesn't sound like your average concussion.

"When she arrived, we knew right away it was very serious. We have been running multiple tests on her brain and we had to perform an emergency brain procedure. She is currently unconscious and a coma has been induced, to try and help decrease some of the swelling on the brain," the doctor added. "We are going to run several more tests in the next couple days. These tests will indicate how much, if any, brain activity she has. I will be here again tomorrow morning, bright and early, to let you know if there are any updates. You can go visit her in the room in a couple hours if you want. I must warn you though—she looks quite a bit different. We had to shave part of her head where the injury occurred."

"This has to be a dream!" I yelled out.

Everybody was in complete and utter shock, sobbing, and the tears that had manifested in my eyes spilled over along with theirs. My anxiety spiked and I felt sick to my stomach. I was dizzy as hell, as if I had just gotten off one of the spinning rides at the fair.

"We have to stay positive everybody." My dad tried to comfort the group.

"All we can really do right now, is sit and wait," Damon added.

"I need to go for a walk," I announced to the group. Damon followed and we walked out of the conference room. We took the elevator down and left the hospital. A good two minutes went by and Damon and I had not yet said a word. We both stared at the ground, puzzled.

"How the hell could this happen to our family?" I asked

"Mom doesn't deserve this. Nobody deserves this,"

Damon said.

Never in my life did I think we'd ever be put into this position. I didn't know what to do, so I cried—something inside of me just felt the need for tears. While we didn't know exactly what was going to happen, none of us had a good feeling about the situation.

"It still feels like this is all a bad dream," Damon said. "If feels like I have left my body and now I'm looking down on us. Looking down from a nightmare."

"Yes, I feel the same way," I stated. "Let's go back inside to the room."

Before I made my way back into the hospital and into the room, I needed to make a phone call. I needed to call my friend Sam.

Sam had been my best friend since I was seventeen. He went to a rival high school, but I first met him at the Hillsdale College basketball camp when we were in fifth grade. We played on the same team that year and instantaneously hit it off.

I hadn't ever made a call like this before. Sam knew me better than anyone did. We talked on the phone pretty much every day.

"What's up, man?" I asked. "What are you doing?"

"Just working," Sam replied. "What are you up to?"

At this point, my voice was wavering and didn't sound like it normally does. I usually have a very confident tone and I'm always saying something funny to Sam when we first address each other. He had never really heard me like this so I knew he could tell that something was wrong.

"What's going on, dude?" Sam asked. "You sound different. Is everything all right?"

I paused for about ten seconds. It took a lot to muster out what I wanted to say. As much pain and agony as I was going through, I still was not comfortable being sad and vulnerable with anyone—not even a best friend who I tell absolutely everything to.

"My mom...she's...she's been in an accident. A bad one. Things aren't looking pretty."

"What?" Sam yelled. "An accident? When? Where? How?"

I paused again and my voice started to quiver. "It happened on US-twelve, dude. Right on our corner. She had just left our house. It happened by the fricken Dairy Treat. It's a damn nightmare. I don't know what the hell we're going to do."

"Is she..." he gasped, "...is she going to be okay?"

"We have no idea. We have no clue. We just talked to the doctors and they didn't say much. Everything is up in the air right now. Right now, she is in a coma. They're running a bunch of tests and will continue tomorrow. It's crazy, man. I was the last one that spoke to her. I was getting ready to go out and she borrowed my car. She was on her way to Walmart to grab a few things. She said she would be right back."

I was on the verge of bawling my eyes out and I didn't want my best friend to hear me like this. I didn't yet realize that it was okay to cry, be emotional or vulnerable. "I gotta go, bro," I said.

"Shit, I don't know what to say. You guys will be in my thoughts and prayers. If you need anybody to talk to, just let me know. Don't hesitate to call for me anything. I don't care if it's three o'clock in the morning. You know I stay up late anyway."

"Thanks," I whispered into the phone. "I will."

The night was getting later as we all sat in the visitors' room for the ICU unit. The pungent smells of disinfectant, medicine, disease and death infiltrated the air. We had been sitting there for two hours and it felt like an eternity. We were still waiting to see what was going to happen. I remember looking at Taryn and Damon. The expressions that were on their faces are something that I could never forget.

Our whole lives flashed before my eyes. I thought of us celebrating birthdays as a family. I thought of our trips to Milham Park in Kalamazoo and the geese we threw bread to there. Damon chasing Taryn and me towards the bridge. We used to race and see who could reach it the fastest. I always won, but that is only because I was the oldest and biggest. I remembered going to Jackson to watch a movie or go out to eat. The road trips we took up north or the vacations we took to Florida and Myrtle Beach. The drives down were always an experience in themselves.

That's what happens when your whole family consists of a bunch of comedians trying to out-do each other. I swear Damon, my Dad and I could all do stand up. We made the most out of those long drives to Lakeland from Michigan to visit my Grandma and Grandpa Krohn at their winter home. All of the family get-togethers at Grandma Langs' house, the time we spent laughing, joking around, swimming in our pool, playing sports—it all came fresh to my mind as if it were just yesterday.

I thought about all this stuff that night. We'd had so many great memories, but I wondered if there would ever be any more with all five of us together. I quivered at the thought.

It was now midnight and we were still sitting in silence. I had pushed two chairs together and sprawled myself over them. We all just lay there that night and it was the same story the next few days.

In the afternoons, I would sit back in the common room of the ICU—it had become our *de facto* property, based on the sheer number of us camped out there. It had been three days in the hospital and I still hadn't eaten anything, despite everyone's insistence. I don't think Taryn, Damon or my dad had either. In fact, I was so sick of the questions about my food intake that I started to lie about it.

People were visiting us left and right, a few of the people I didn't even know. Some of my close friends from high school and college called me and offered their support. For the most part, I couldn't talk on the phone though. I just didn't feel up to it even though I appreciated all the well-wishers and people offering condolences.

We had been there for five days now and the doctor had an announcement to make in the morning. The nurses had told us he would stop by early to share his news. This gave us a reason to be cheerful. We thought he was going to share good news with us, and my family started to talk about how we were going to live when Mom woke up and got back to normal. We talked about how we were going to visit each other more often. No longer would weeks go by without visiting our house in Jonesville. We were all incredibly busy, but that didn't matter. We would make it work.

That night we all had a pleasant sleep. My family consists of a bunch of eternal optimists so we were looking forward to the positive news. We knew it would be a long road to recovery, but we expected her to awake from the coma and eventually come back to her usual self.

The next morning we woke up, showered and got ready to meet with the doctor. We were still in the ICU unit, but in a special meeting room. Everybody was there and we were patiently waiting.

I still remember what I was wearing. A pair of khaki shorts and a red-and-blue Detroit Pistons shirt. We all made small talk, anxiously awaiting the doctor. I was excited for a change—I thought there was just more than a glimmer of hope that my mom would survive this—but I was also nervous as hell.

I could feel the room tense up as the doctor walked in. His face was unreadable. He sat in front of all us with two nurses by his side.

This can't be good. This guy should at least have a hint of a smile on his face if the news was good.

"Good morning, everybody. I'm not going to beat around the bush. What we've determined based on a large number of different tests that Patricia has been given over the course of the last few days—it's not good. I would say the chances of her waking up from this coma are less than two percent. And most likely, if she ever did wake up, she would be in a vegetative state."

My back slid down in my seat and I started crying harder than I'd ever cried in my whole entire life. An intense sensation of heat emanated from my body, but I was freezing cold. I trembled so violently, I'm surprised the doctor didn't stop and treat me for having a seizure. My heart was beating hard. I felt numb. I wanted to feel something—I ached tremendously to feel some sense of denial and resentment. I wanted, even for a minute, to believe that everything was okay and my mom was going to survive this.

But I knew.

I knew she wasn't going to make it. I knew it wasn't going to be okay.

Everybody shared those sentiments. My whole family was crying. Even people I had never seen cry, were crying.

I heard a family member sob, "This isn't fair. This is just not right."

We all took our turns going into my mom's room to say goodbye. I wept so hard I thought I would never stop. There was a preacher in the room saying prayers. We all gathered in that cold, numb, dead room and cried.

How could this be her reality? This wasn't right. She was supposed to grow old with my dad and she was supposed to watch us all graduate and see us get married. She was the best mother in the world. She would have made the best grandmother too. She was only forty-seven years old.

I sat next to her, kissed her hand and kissed her cheek. I kissed her forehead. I had told her that I loved her about a hundred times over that last week—I said it again. I wished I'd said it more in the past. In my mind, I really would like to believe that she heard me while lying in that bed.

"It's time to let her go," my dad said.

We couldn't let my mom be a vegetable. My mom was *Super Woman*. Even if she ever did wake up, she would never in a million years want to live like a vegetable. My mother was the most independent woman I've ever met in my life, even to this day. Not only did she work full-time at an elementary school, she cooked in the evening, did the dishes and cleaned up after all of us. She ironed our clothes, made us breakfast in the morning and did the majority of the yard work when it was needed.

Who fixed the garbage deposal when it went down? *My mom*.

Who fixed the lawnmower went it wouldn't run? *My mom*.

Who put my gigantic bed together in college—the one I couldn't figure out if my life depended on it? *My mom.*

This wasn't a knock against my dad, but Mom was the *handyman* around the house. Dad would say the exact same thing. Matter of fact, he would laugh about it. I don't know how to fix anything either. To this day, my wife is the one that handles all of the handy stuff. She can fix things and I can't. It's just like how my mom and dad were.

My mom loved us more than anything in the world and she was so proud of Taryn, Damon and me. She spent most of her time taking care of us. She knew that we loved her, but I couldn't help but think that I should have said it more. I should have helped her around the house more. I should have helped her clean the house more than I did. For God's sake, I shouldn't have complained about raking the leaves or mowing the yard.

All I had were memories now. The last time I saw my mom and dad together, they were hugging and kissing in the kitchen. They were so affectionate with each other. I had so many fond memories of my mom. And now my final memory is of her lying in a hospital bed, dying.

That isn't fair. How could I get this image out of my mind? I didn't want this to be the way I remembered her.

Chapter Nine
The Funeral

"It's time to get up, Ryan." My dad opened the basement door and called from the top of the stairs.

"Okay, Dad. I'm up. I'm up," I said. "I'll shower in five minutes."

I couldn't believe the day was here. It was a day that I thought wouldn't happen until I was at least fifty years old. However, I am only twenty-one and we have to bury my mom. The most significant person in my life was about to leave us for good. It would be the last time we see her in the physical. I walked up the stairs. Our house had a very empty feeling in it—a feeling that has remained ever since the accident.

My dad was already dressed and ready to go. He was anxious, pacing back and forth the living room.

It was time for me to get in the shower. As the hot water bounced off my neck and tingled down my spine, my thoughts began to drift. I imagined myself in a faraway place with nothing but peace and tranquility. This world ceased to exist and I was relaxing for the first time in over a week. My family and I were lying at the beach. The tide was coming in, waves were crashing and sea gulls could be heard in the distance. I heard children playing in the water and as each wave hit, I took a breath. I was dozing off in my perfect world and I was happy knowing my family was close by. *Ah. This feels nice.*

The door knocks, "Ryan, let's go." I opened my eyes a split second after I heard my dad's voice. *Damn!* Back to reality and this infinite sadness that has consumed me and my family for the last week.

"Okay, Dad, just a minute."

So much for peace and tranquility. Usually, when I got out of the shower, my body was hot. I would often open the bathroom door as soon as the shower ended to let the steam out. This time it was different—I had just gotten out of a hot shower and I was freezing cold. Furthermore, my chest had felt cold for the last week. It didn't matter how hot it was outside or how hot the shower was. I felt so cold and weak on the inside and this feeling had a firm grasp on my whole body and soul.

Putting on dress clothes was typically something that I enjoyed. This wasn't going to be one of those times. I put on a black dress shirt, a gray tie and a brand-new pair of gray slacks. I looked sharp, but it didn't matter.

My dad, Taryn, Damon and I reconvened in the kitchen when it was time to go. Honestly, I was half tempted to guzzle the remainder of beers from the night before to ease some of the pain. But that wouldn't be a good idea.

My mother's funeral was being held at the high school. We had to have it there because the funeral home itself wouldn't be able to hold the amount of people that were expected. The funeral director had told me a couple of days prior that he had never seen a visitation with as many people as my mom's. People had come from everywhere. When the visitation began, the line was out the door and fanning out about a half mile.

Being an elementary school counselor for years, she was widely known throughout the community. Everybody loved her and wanted to get to know her. My mom's death rocked our little community.

With all that being said, the high school gymnasium

was one of the biggest places in the whole town so it was an ideal location to house a few hundred people. Considering my mother was an educator herself, it also seemed rather fitting for it to be held there.

When we showed up there was already a huge crowd. It was a dreary day but I was not going to succumb to it. I was going to try to pull through the best I could. My mom always said there was going to be plenty of stuff that I'd have to do in life that I didn't want to. This was one of the things. My best bet was to suck it up and get through it.

We parked by the side of the school. "Well, guys, let's go," my dad said. "Time to go in."

We walked into the side door. As much as I'd had my days where I didn't want to go through that door to go to school, none compared to this time. I just didn't want to see anybody that I knew, other than family.

Over the course of the last several days, I had only talked to a few people outside of my family. I knew I would see them today, but I didn't really want them to see me like this. Nobody had ever seen me vulnerable and miserable. My body was an entanglement of nerves, sadness and despair. I knew people would be feeling awkward around me. For them to see me not smiling and joking around would be a shock, as that was all anybody saw out of me—until this point in my life.

It was cold and dreary as we walked down the hallway to the JHS band room. I glanced around and saw mostly family and close friends of my mom. There were approximately thirty people in the room. I remembered walking down that hallway to get to my locker in seventh grade.

A friend of hers spoke to me at the funeral and told me that my mom had a very unique ability. The woman was an elementary school counselor herself and admitted to me that she couldn't do all the things that my mom could do. She said that my mom had the ability to read the kids and really empathize with them. That was so true. My mom cared about her students so much and it was obvious when witnessing how the kids reacted when they saw her.

I remember going to one of Damon's football games during his junior year. We got stopped about a dozen times walking from our van to the stands. It seemed like every time we saw a little kid they would come up to my mom and want to give her a hug. They were there to watch Damon play and support my mom. She always thanked the kids for coming to our games.

Her relationship with the students she counseled was strong. She taught them respect by giving them respect. Whether at school or out in the community, she would always take time out to chat with them and she wouldn't just make small talk. She genuinely cared.

Many of the students that she dealt with didn't have a good parent as a role model. They didn't have anybody at home to guide them. They saw my mom as more than a a counselor—they saw her as a friend and a parent figure.

I remembered the winter of 2001, right after Damon's football season had ended. It was the last Christmas I ever experienced with my mom. I was twenty years old and home for winter vacation. It was a Thursday night, we had just finished dinner and I was getting ready to go to Sam's house. Mom asked me to go shopping with her. She wanted to go to Walmart, and although it was convenient and close, I wasn't a big fan.

I didn't want to go, but I could see my mom wanted me to, so I asked her why she wanted to go there.

"I need to get some toys and clothes for a group of underprivileged kids that our foundation sponsors." My mother was a proud member of the Jonesville Community

Educational Foundation. "The Wilson family has nothing after the fire. We need to make sure we help out as much as possible."

This would take away from hanging out with my best friend, but it was for a great cause. Having had a relatively easy life so far, I could sympathize but I couldn't empathize the way my mom could.

"Okay, I'll go with you," I said.

So I joined my mom at Walmart. We picked out tons of toys and copious amounts of clothes for a few different families. We were in that store for at least a couple hours.

She led by example that night. I truly learned what it meant to be generous and giving. It brought such joy to Mom's face to pick out the toys for those kids. She couldn't wait until Christmas time so she could shower them with gifts.

I was so proud that she was my mother, and I felt guilty and ashamed that I had contemplated being selfish just a couple of hours before and going to my friend's house instead of going to help her out. She taught me what it was like to be humble and gracious. Although I was appreciative of what my parents gave me, it never hurts to have a little reminder of what it takes to be humble.

Now, in the aftermath of my mom's death, no matter how angry I get I will never forget how to treat people— the way our beloved Red taught me.

The funeral service was still a half hour away. We had just thirty minutes to say goodbye. My mom's body lay in the casket. She was wearing her favorite purple blazer. There were flower displays and plants lined up throughout the perimeter of the room and the somber look on everyone's face told the story.

I had never seen so many tissue boxes in my life. My aunt and grandma were crying along with some relatives that I didn't even know. My mom had a lot of cousins, aunts and uncles that I had only met a time or two. Even though I didn't really know them, it was nice to see all the support. They obviously all loved my mom as well.

I couldn't believe it was time to say goodbye. I hugged all my family members. We all said the same thing. We loved my mom more than anything in the world. My dad, Taryn, Damon and I walked over to the casket.

My dad put his hand on my mom's face. "Your spirit will live on through your kids," he said to her with solace in his voice. "They will always love you and you will always be a part of them. I'll love you forever."

The lyrics from the song "Fix you" by Coldplay ring true in my head as I remember this moment head on with full force.

"I love you, Mom." I muster out these four words with all my might. Taryn and Damon do the same. "You'll always be with us in everything that we do. You'll be in our hearts forever."

Ten more minutes passed and it was time to gather to the gym for the funeral service. The pastor came in to check on us and tell us it was time to start. The pallbearers picked up the casket and walked out of the room. They proceeded to carry it to the front of the gym. My mom's closest friends left.

Now it was time for the family to line up. We all lined up beginning with my dad and Damon. Taryn came after with my Aunt Shari and I brought up the rear. I took a deep breath as we walked out of the band room.

This was one of the longest walks of my life. It was only a couple hundred feet to the gym but I was a little dizzy. I could hear horns playing. I had this buzzing sound going through my head. It was the lyrics to my favorite song ever. The song "Dance" by Nas.

I can't even begin to tell you how many times I listened to this song the week after my mom died. The lyrics are burned to my mind. But I had to push it away for fear of completely losing it in front of a packed gymnasium. It was hard for me to keep my head up but I looked straight ahead as I followed my family members to our seats in the front row. It was time to start the funeral service.

The pastor came out and addressed the crowd. "Hello everyone. We are here not to mourn of the loss of a friend, but to celebrate the life of a friend. Patricia Dorene Langs Krohn was a mother, a wife, a teacher, a counselor, a neighbor, a friend and an inspiration to all of us. She was one of the most generous people I have ever had the privilege of knowing. She went out of her way to help others in need. She wasn't happy until everybody was happy."

These words rang true in my head. I have known this my whole life. No one loved and supported me more than my mother.

For instance, when I was in college I had very lofty goals—I wanted to be somebody special. I wanted to make a difference. It wasn't about the money, but I wanted to make lots of it so I could provide for my whole family one day. That was my motivation for wanting to be a chiropractor.

Nonetheless, I had doubts that I could accomplish this. Truthfully, I had never been very good with science and math, so I guess I was naive to think I could pass it in college. Something needed to give. My mom always supported me and said that if I really wanted it, I could have it. So, although chiropractic school didn't work out, knowing that my mom supported and believed in me is what mattered.

Sitting there, as the words churned out of the pastor's mouth, I couldn't believe it was going to be the last time I would see my mother.

When the funeral procession finished, it was time to drive to the cemetery, time to lay my mom in her final resting place.

My dad, Taryn, Damon and I hopped in our car and followed the hearse carrying my mom's body. The cemetery was only a mile from the high school so it was a short trip and none of us really said anything.

We arrived and got out of the car. With every step towards her gravesite, I realized we were getting that much closer to the inevitable—that we would never see my mom in the flesh again.

Many of our friends and family were already there. A few buddies of mine from college who I hadn't seen in a while showed up. You definitely find out who your true friends are during a time of need.

There were chairs lined up into three rows behind the site and the casket was on a metal gurney right above the freshly dug hole. The pastor showed up and led us in a few short prayers. Most of my family had tears in their eyes. A few of them were bawling their eyes out. The final prayer was said in unison and the casket was dropped in its final resting place. It was time to say goodbye.

Chapter Ten
Coping Mechanisms

In every death, a new life for the loved ones left behind is created whether we like it or not. There comes a point in time when we have to decide whether we are going to move on or stay put. Will we let the feeling of our loved one's non-existence consume our thoughts and emotions, or will the manifestation of their spiritual being provide sufficient means to face life in the aftermath of their departure?

The effects of death can influence a person in a number of ways. How you let it shape your life could be the difference between happiness and depression. I came to the point where I simply couldn't live the same life I had been living. Dealing with the death of my mom has been the toughest thing I have ever endured. Nothing else comes close, even though I have been through many trials and tribulations since her passing.

Losing the number one person in my life has left a huge void in my soul. It's like going to bed dreaming of waking up to sunshine, only to open your eyes to a gloomy, rainy day—every day.

For instance, picture a little child who is looking forward to Christmas morning. Although the child knows the true meaning of Christmas, he is expecting a ton of presents, a reward for his excellent behavior all year. The child wakes up. Christmas is here! He runs to the living room with a huge smile on his face, ready for a very special day. But, wait...nothing is there.

What has happened? Where are all the presents? Is this for real? Santa has forgotten about him. He is sad and he begins to weep uncontrollably. He runs to his parents' room. There's nobody there. What's going on? Is this a dream? The child pinches himself and runs back to his bedroom. Yes, the mouse is on the twenty-fifth. It is December. This is Christmas morning. It's not a dream.

His world has been turned upside down. Maybe Christmas will come another day. He still has hope.

For me, waking up, I felt like that small child every day after losing my mom. Except, with death there is no other day, no next time. No hope. Not in this lifetime—maybe in the next if such a thing exists. But in this life, I had to live every day knowing that I will never see her again.

For many months, this feeling of emptiness consumed my every thought and emotion—it consumed *me*. Every reminder of the tragedy accentuated my feelings of loneliness and despair. I lived with a perpetual sick feeling in the pit of my stomach. But even though I was going through my own problems, I still put a smile on my face. Although smiling does not necessarily mean you're happy. Sometimes it just means that you're strong. I was very good at masking my sadness and depression. When I did hang out with friends and family, I acted happy and people bought it.

If you were to look at the random collage of pictures from these days, you might conclude that I was the happiest dude on the planet. This couldn't be further from the truth. I was absolutely miserable.

See, it didn't hit me right away. Matter of fact, my anxiety, depression and loneliness didn't manifest themselves fully until a few years after her death. Right after my mom passed away, I felt the need to be very strong and positive. My whole family was extremely strong because that is just in our nature. It is the way we were raised.

A lot of friends and family were really sad and disillusioned with my mom's death. Some people close to me even questioned the existence of God. They wondered if there really was a God, or if there was, how He could take a saint like my mother. So many people said that my mother was one of the best people that they ever had the pleasure of knowing. They all wanted to know what kind of God would take my mother.

With religious views aside, I stayed positive about the whole situation. I was still in shock immediately following her death, but I offered a helping hand to those in need and I reached out to people who wanted to talk about it. I told them there is a God and that God needed a counselor to help with little children in heaven. I told them she was in heaven, with God now, and that she was safe and at peace.

These words of encouragement seemed to help people a lot. At least, they seemed at ease when I gave them my thoughts and opinions on things. At this point, I was still the happy-go-lucky kid that everyone knew me to be, always optimistic about life in general. After all, that was what I had been taught from my mom.

My Grandpa Langs passed away on June 7, 1988. I was only seven and my mom was only thirty-three at the time of her father's passing.

She got the call about her Dad passing away, in the middle of the night. My Grandpa Langs had had some health problems stemming from blood clots and poor circulation. He had been hooked up to an oxygen tank.

I awoke that night to my mom and dad crying. My room was very close to theirs so it wasn't hard to hear them. I heard them crying for a few minutes and then I heard my mom get dressed and leave our house. She went over to my grandma's house, only a couple blocks away.

At the age of seven, I didn't really know what death was. I was on the couch the next morning when my mom walked back into our house. I asked her about Grandpa Langs. She wasn't crying anymore and she looked okay.

"Grandpa Langs passed away last night," Mom said. "He went to heaven."

Even though she had told me that he had died, I don't think I fully comprehended that he wasn't coming back.

My dad sat us down and told Taryn, Damon and me that it was going to be a very tough couple of weeks for our mom. We needed to behave and let her take it easy.

My mom stayed strong, for everybody in the family, during her father's death. My grandfather had been a well-liked and respected businessman in the community, and everybody loved him. A lot of people were going to miss him. My mom was strong for her sister and brothers. She was also there for my Grandma Langs, who had just lost the love of her life.

Grandpa Langs was only sixty-three years old when he died, which is still fairly young. My mom told us that life wasn't always fair and that my grandpa had taught her that.

Nobody knows why a good person dies at a young age. We don't know why children get cancer and we don't know why good people die in horrible accidents. But such is life, and sometimes it isn't fair.

Some people can smoke and drink their whole life and live to be ninety. Other people might run five miles a day; never drink or smoke and die of cancer at thirty-five. It's sad and confusing when that happens, but unfortunately, it is sometimes a fact of life. All we can do is be the best person we can be for our family and loved ones, but when it's our time, it's our time. That is just the way it is.

My mom was always levelheaded and a very rational thinker. She'd learned the definition of great family ethics from her parents, and she certainly did her best to pass them on to her own children.

She'd lived a happy life after my grandpa passed away. Some people are simply better at dealing with adversity than others are. Although, I know there were times when she hurt and she kept it to herself. She was always able to talk about my grandpa with a smile on her face and she would tell us funny stories about him.

After my mom's passing, I made the decision to change my major from biochemistry to psychology. I wanted to help people. I wanted to be like my mom.

Being a counselor as she was, or even having my own private practice, was something that I wanted. I had just finished my junior year at WMU at the time of the accident, so by this point, I had completed all of my general education requirements and I just needed to start taking psychology courses.

After speaking with my advisor, I realized I could complete all the necessary classes in under two years. With that being said, I would be on pace to graduate after my fifth year at Western. *Ahhh! That dreaded fifth year—I would be a fifth year senior.* At first, I was a little embarrassed to admit it, but then I learned that this is very common. Matter of fact, it is more common nowadays to take more than four years. Hell, I know a lot of people that took six or seven years. There is absolutely nothing wrong with that either.

College is a time to explore your options and learn

who you are as a person. It's very common to change your mind a few times before settling on something. I had switched my mind three times when I had finally settled on becoming a psychology major.

During my last two years of college, I was extremely busy writing papers, completing a practicum helping adults with special needs and constructing various PowerPoint presentations relating to specific material in those classes. Between all this, my classes, my girlfriend at the time and playing intramural sports, I was as busy as ever. But being busy kept me from really thinking about the loss of my mom too much. Occasionally, I would have a night when I would break down and cry for a while. Mostly, I was too busy and too tired to let it affect me.

I graduated from Western Michigan University on April 24, 2004. It was a glorious day. A day I had been looking forward to since I graduated from high school in 1999. I felt relieved and joyous that all my hard work had finally paid off. My family would be there and some of my friends and fellow graduates would be participating in the event as well.

Despite being happy and proud of my accomplishments, I couldn't help but realize this would be a very bittersweet afternoon— my mom wasn't going to be there.

I felt a sense of being ripped-off because she wouldn't get to see it in person. Thousands of people would clap and holler as we walked across the stage, but the one person that I wanted to have see me walk that walk, wouldn't be there. I knew she was looking down on me from above, though. People live for these very special moments. When you can't share them with all the people you love, it hurts.

After all, she was the reason I went into psychology,

81

the reason I wanted to help people—all people. It was because of her. I loved the reaction she got when she knew she had made a real difference and I wanted to emulate that. I wanted to have the same influence on people, make the same kind of difference.

Regardless of the disappointment I felt inside my soul, at least my dad, brother and sister would still be there. This made me smile. Being the oldest sibling, I felt that I needed to help set a good example. Although Taryn and Damon didn't really need any guidance as far as graduating from college. With that being said, I knew that graduating college was a path that I was expected to take and I could feel proud about leading the way for my little sister and brother.

It was a warm day. I put on my best blue button-up shirt and khaki pants. We drove to campus and I went backstage to get ready for the ceremony.

The auditorium was a huge sea of black. Everybody had donned a black cap and gown. I lined up the tassel on my cap, took a seat and waited my turn, surrounded by a bunch of other people whose last name started with K.

The time to hit the stage came. I stood with pride, remembering that this was the same place Mom and Dad had stood, preparing to graduate and take on the world. The same place my Grandpa and Grandma Krohn had met, fallen in love and graduated from—my Aunt Janis too. Wow. What a feeling. That was the central reason I decided to go to WMU in the first place. I almost went to Michigan State, or I could have gone to Olivet and played basketball, but none that felt right. This felt right.

I waited with anticipation for my last name to be called and I stood there basking in the glow, with a big smile on my face. The auditorium had two very large levels and I knew that my family was way up at the top watching down on me. But as high as they were, there would be somebody higher up watching over me. In my heart of hearts, I knew that Mom was watching down over me from heaven. She had to be. I could feel it.

The President of the University called out, "Graduating with a major in psychology and a minor in sociology, Ryan Matthew Krohn."

I walked to the front of the stage and I shook the president's hand, along with three other people I didn't really know. The moment only lasted about ten seconds, but when I looked up and saw a sea of people, it was pretty cool—all eyes were on me. I hadn't really experienced anything like that before.

Then I walked off the stage and sat back down. And that was that. I was officially a Western Michigan University graduate. Time to move on with my life.

Chapter Eleven
Post Graduation

Now that I was officially a college graduate, it was time to start thinking about the next step. Where would I go from here? In most cases, it's extremely hard to find a job right after college. This would most definitely be the case with me. Maybe especially with me. Because graduating with a degree in psychology is often just a stepping-stone for obtaining a job in the field. I knew this, but sometimes I liked to forget. Furthering my education would be paramount if I really wanted to achieve something great in this field—I needed to get my master's degree in counseling psychology.

In order to achieve this, I needed thirty-nine credits. That would take me approximately three years. *Damn.* Three more years. I didn't know if I had that kind of patience.

One of my best friends was doing the exact same thing. He was a few years older than I was, and he was almost done with the program. After graduating with his master's in psych, he got accepted into Western's counseling psych program. He was able to dedicate all of his time to his master's and it still took him about three years.

Because most people had jobs, all of the classes were scheduled in the late afternoon and evening. The earliest class was scheduled at four o'clock p.m. Even so, this wasn't a very popular and common choice among students seeking their master's. Most of the classes started at six or six thirty p.m. and would typically go until eight thirty or nine o'clock, twice a week. I was relieved not to have any more early morning classes.

Since I didn't have a job right after college, applying to graduate school seemed like my smartest option. My friend, Greg, gave me a few tips on applying to the Counseling Psychology Program. I knew that I needed to get three reliable sources and Greg pointed me in the right direction. His experience would come in handy.

I may not have been applying to Harvard or Yale, but WMU's Counseling Psychology Department was still highly revered nationwide. I needed to write a very convincing letter to the admissions department.

So, after accumulating the necessary sources from various professors, it was time to write my letter. I needed to hit a homerun with this thing. Not many people would be accepted into this program, but considering I already had my undergraduate degree from WMU, I had an advantage. Universities tend to grab people that had previously attended their institution. However, while graduating with a 3.2 Grade Point Average isn't bad, there would most likely be a lot of people with better credentials—most have at least a 3.5.

I thought long and hard about what I wanted to say. It had to be something special. Something that would separate me from the pack. The answer hit me right in the face. I could talk about my mom and tell them about her being a counselor, how it influenced me. I would tell them I was made for this.

I would use Mom's tragedy to show them how this experience would allow me to not only sympathize but also empathize with clients. I would explain how the things I learned from her, and from her death, shaped me into the perfect candidate. This would make me a very effective counselor. I needed to take all those feelings of loneliness and despair and channel them into my Purpose Letter. Being able to convey these thoughts and emotions to my reader would be my ticket to securing a spot in the program. Even though she was no longer here, my mother would still inspire, support and help me succeed.

Waiting on the response of the WMU Board of Admissions took a lot of my time. I rented an apartment at Drake's Pond and the rent was much steeper that I was used to. I got a one-bedroom apartment on purpose because I wanted to try out living by myself for a change. I'd had roommates in all my years in college so the rent and bills were always split up accordingly. So now, while I was working towards my career, I needed to find a job that would at least pay the bills.

I decided to apply at a pharmaceutical research company that a friend worked at. The position was in quality assurance and I would audit research the scientists were working on. It didn't really sound like my cup of tea at all. Nevertheless, I had the hook-up with my buddy so getting a position there seemed attainable. The job paid fifteen dollars an hour, so it was almost double from the eight dollars an hour I was used to in college.

A couple weeks went by and I was still waiting to hear back from the company. I love time off so I spent it very leisurely. My day consisted of waking up at noon, playing basketball at the park and then usually going out somewhere at night. I lived in close proximity to a lot of restaurants and bars. I would go out with some of my younger friends that were still working on their undergraduate. We would watch the Pistons play and enjoy a few beers. It felt nice to relax a bit. I knew I would be busy again shortly though.

I finally received a call from the pharmaceutical

company to come in for an interview. I was pretty pumped because the possibility of making fifteen dollars an hour eased my mind. That morning I dressed in a nice Ralph Lauren suit and practiced potential questions in the mirror. I wasn't very worried about the interview because I always did really well in those types of situations.

I can be a very charming and charismatic person when I want to be and impressing someone has never been a problem. I'm very good at saying what people want to hear. I can bullshit with the best of them.

The interview went really well and I was hired on spot. It's not as if I needed a PhD in chemistry to obtain this position, but I did need to have some background in the field. Who would have thought my two years as a biochemistry major would actually help me?

Chapter Twelve
Florida Relocation

It was the fall of 2005 and I needed a change in my life. I was sick of the mundane world to which I had been accustomed. It seemed like the same old thing. Sure, I loved seeing my family and best friends a lot, but it got to the point where unequivocal change needed to happen in my life in order for me to feel satisfied. Feeling malcontent was just something I wouldn't put up with. Life is short and I didn't want to spend one second feeling unhappy.

At this point, I had only been working a real job for a few months. On top of that, I had just dived into my master's program. It would be heartbreaking to tell my professors I was leaving, but I concluded that it needed to be done.

When I walked into one of my professor's offices, he could tell something was up. He was a real good guy. From New York City, he'd been a professor at WMU for several years. In his mid-forties, African-American, he had long dreads and a long beard to go with it. Unlike a lot of professors, he was very easy to talk with.

"I really appreciate your class and what you have done for me," I said, with hesitation. "But ultimately, at this point in my life, I need to venture on and try something else. I thought this was what I wanted, but I recently changed my mind. I want to move somewhere and explore myself. I quit my job, my girl and now I'm going to quit this program. Since my mom passed away,

I've realized just how fragile life can be. You only live once and I'm going to live mine to the fullest."

He looked at me with a glow in his eyes. "I saw something unique in you the first time I met you," he said. "I could feel the love and passion in your voice when you talked about your mom. You just want to make her proud. I see something very special down the road for you. You want to make a positive impact on people. You want to change their thinking. You want to change their whole existence for living. Maybe this isn't what you are supposed to be doing. Sounds like you have some soul searching to do. It may take awhile, but you will find your real purpose one day."

My eyes welled up as he ended. He had such a great way with words. In my heart of hearts, I knew these things, but I needed to hear him say it too. "Thanks for the kind words," I said. I still felt a little awestruck. This guy was highly respected in the counseling world. "Hopefully, I'll see you again one day."

"Keep in touch, Ryan," he said. "Let me know what you decide. Remember it may take you several years to find your purpose in this world, but you will."

I had recently become single. It was a mutual break-up. She had been there for me after my mom's death and the immediate aftermath of that. While I greatly appreciated the love and support, it just came to the point where we grew apart. We wanted to go in different directions. I told her I wanted to leave Michigan. She wanted to stay. When you're unconditionally in love with someone, you'll make it happen. It didn't seem like either of us were in that boat, so we knew it was time to move on. Why settle for something you're not happy with? I deserved to be happy. I needed to go all out.

I had always been a risk taker. My mom's death taught me to live life to the fullest, and living in Michigan for twenty-five years, I knew one thing. I wanted to get out of the cold. I wanted to go somewhere that was sunny and warm for most of the year.

I had been looking at various places online and it boiled down to two choices. Either somewhere down south or out west.

I had been to Florida numerous times with my family. Also, some of my buddies and I went to the Tampa area the previous year for spring break. I really enjoyed my trip there. The warmer temperatures were very appealing to me. I loved the weather, the scenery and the oceans. Florida was also a hell of a lot closer to Michigan than California was. The cost of living wasn't near as bad as places in California either.

The culmination of all these things resulted in me choosing Tampa. I was doing it on a whim. I didn't have a job lined up, but I didn't care. And I didn't care if anybody was going with me either. However, it would be nice if somebody did. I had known a couple possibilities of people that might be interested in moving. One of my good buddies from college, Brian, would be a solid candidate. I proposed the idea to him. He knew my situation and that I wanted to leave Michigan. He was living with me at my apartment in Kalamazoo and he was up for anything. Brian was looking for jobs in the area, but he wasn't having much luck. He had some money saved up as well, so he was highly interested in moving somewhere.

One night, a couple weeks before Christmas, we were just sitting at the apartment drinking a few beers. We were conversing about our problems and frustrations when I announced, "Fuck it, dude. Let's move to Tampa. We

90

went there last year for spring break and loved it. What's the worst that could happen? We live down there for a few months or a year, and if it doesn't work out we can move back."

"Really?" he asked. "You're that serious about this huh?"

"Why the hell not, man? We're both about to turn twenty-five. We're single. We have nothing holding us back here. Sure it sort of sucks to live far away from family, but we can visit them whenever we want. I'm going to do it whether you are or not."

"You're right," he said, agreeing with my little tirade. "I don't really have anything holding me back here. When would you want to move?"

"Well considering it's December, I would like to move in a month or two. Let's move in early February. That way we'll at least be missing most of the winter here."

"Okay, so what day?" he asked.

I grabbed my Detroit Pistons calendar and looked at the upcoming dates. "Well the Super Bowl is February fifth and we'll probably be hung over the next day—so, Tuesday it is. February seventh, Florida here we come."

We had the date we were going to move and that still gave me a month and a half to hang out with family and some of my best friends. Some were sad I was leaving. Others were very happy for me. My family sincerely wished me the best, although I didn't really think my dad believed I was leaving. I remember talking to Taryn one night and she told me that my dad asked her if I really was serious about it.

Dad's skepticism was fully warranted, because I was notorious for switching my mind. It was only a few months ago that I declared that I wanted to go all the way and get my doctorate degree. The good news was, my dad was happy I decided to make a change. Once he realized I was ready for a change, he supported me wholeheartedly.

February 7 arrived and I felt like a little kid at Christmas time. I was elated it was finally time to venture on and move on with my life. Brian showed up bright and early at seven a.m. with the U-haul trailer. It was attached to the back of his SUV. It actually looked small until you opened it and walked in. We didn't have much furniture, yet it was absolutely necessary we had it for this trip.

Our vehicles were filled to the very brim. Taryn and my dad helped me pile up the Camaro with boxes of clothes, pictures, cleaning supplies and other miscellaneous things that were scattered across my bedroom floor. Thankfully, the heaviest things we carried down were my mattress along with the box spring and bed frame. After we got the table and chairs in the trailer, we were ready for the long haul.

It was two o'clock in the afternoon and it had started to snow like crazy. Great timing. I was a seasoned veteran when it came down to driving in the snow so I wasn't too worried.

"Make sure you're careful driving," Taryn said, in a worrisome tone.

"Yeah don't drive too crazy out there, Ryan," my dad added.

"I'll be fine guys, I'm driving down to Lexington and staying at Krause's tonight. Tomorrow night we'll arrive in Tampa." I hugged them both and said goodbye. I really didn't know how long it would be until I saw them again. It was a weird feeling because usually I saw them at least every other week.

We hopped in our vehicles and we were off. I wanted

to follow Brian because he had the slower SUV plus the trailer attached to it. I had a tendency to drive a little too fast, as evidenced by the few speeding tickets I had.

We had a long, distant drive ahead of us. As we began our journey, I looked in the rear-view mirror. My reign in Kalamazoo had come to an end. Time to conquer another place.

Chapter Thirteen
Life in Florida

The new beginnings were here. My mind had wandered as I anticipated in amazement what could be in store for us. And then with a surge of eagerness, Brian and I raced to the *Welcome to Florida* sign that could be seen in the distance about five hundred feet away. My little 2002 white Camaro had been following him for the majority of the trip. It was time to pass. "Screw it," I said to myself. "Let's open it up a little bit."

As I pushed down on the gas, the speedometer hit eighty-five. I was inching closer to Brian's SUV. My car wasn't that fast, but it was definitely quicker than his vehicle, especially considering he had a trailer on the end of his. Only a hundred yards to go. I accelerated to ninety and Brian didn't know what hit him. I flipped him off as I raced past. He was smiling and shaking his head. Luckily, there were no cops around. I didn't need another speeding ticket.

We finally reached our destination. About time. The drive wasn't terrible, but if you've never done it you can only imagine how long it is. We were on the road driving for a total of about nineteen and half hours. Considering I was following an SUV with a heavy load, that wasn't bad.

It was dark as hell out. We were going to stay the night at the apartment of one of Brian's friends. It was a familiar place as we stayed there for a week last year for spring break. It felt almost as if we had never left.

The warm Florida air felt great. It was about sixty

degrees that night—much better than the twenty degrees it was in Michigan.

We agreed to stay at Megan's that night and then look for apartments the next day. The Tampa Bay area spreads out for hundreds of miles. We didn't know for sure where we were going to stay. Megan lived in what is known as New Tampa. It was on the north side of Tampa and near the University of South Florida. We liked the area. However, we had something else in mind. We were thinking about Brandon. Brandon is a suburb about ten miles east of downtown Tampa. We liked the location because it was close to downtown and New Tampa. It was a mid-sized town consisting of a population of approximately one hundred thousand people. Brandon is similar to Kalamazoo in size, but it was a little bigger and more commercialized. There were a ton of businesses, restaurants and shopping plazas in the area. Brandon seemed like an excellent location because the traffic wasn't near as crowded as Tampa's traffic.

We woke up bright and early that next morning and began our quest for an apartment. Some may think it's quite ludicrous to be doing this since neither of us had jobs. We didn't care. It was okay in our eyes. This pretty much summed up the way that Brian and I rolled. We we're both very spur of the moment types, plus we both had some money saved up for a rainy day.

We ventured on to Brandon and made a stop at an apartment complex on a busy road. It looked like most of the nice apartment complexes in Brandon. As we drove into the gate, I noticed the cobblestone driveway. We pulled up to the leasing office. The place looked really nice. There were tennis courts, basketball courts and a beautiful swimming pool with a Jacuzzi attached to it. We walked in and were greeted by a buxom lady, probably in her mid forties.

"Hello," she said, with a big smile on her face. "Can I help you?"

"We're looking for an apartment," Brian answered back. "What are your prices?"

She motioned us over to her desk. The lady pulled out some brochures and began to talk to us about all the amenities and luxuries provided at the apartment. It was definitely impressive.

"How much are these?" Brian inquired.

"Depends what you want," she said. "We have different bedrooms and various floor plans to everyone's liking. The two bedroom rooms are going for twelve hundred dollars a month."

"Holy shit!" Brian looked at me with surprise. "Six hundred dollars apiece? I was looking for something a little a little cheaper than that."

I started laughing. Brian couldn't be subtle if his life depended on it.

"Well, we don't need anything too extravagant," I answered back. "Unfortunately, if twelve hundred dollars is the cheapest, I guess we'll have to look elsewhere. Thanks."

I was respectful and polite, but I didn't feel like wasting any more time either. We needed to find a place a little cheaper than that, but we didn't want to live in a bad area either. It wasn't as if Brandon could be compared to Compton or Detroit, but still we were not in Jonesville anymore.

"We can't fucking afford twelve hundred a month," Brian said, with an angry tone.

"Yeah I know. We can find better," I said. "Just relax. We'll find a place before the end of the day."

I was appreciative of Megan's hospitality, but I didn't want to stay there another night. Not because I didn't like it, but rather because she had her own life and I didn't want to be a burden to anyone. We were big boys. We could find a place of our own.

We drove down the road and found a place that looked interesting. It was called Courtney Trails. All we could see from the highway was what looked like a damn palace in the midst of a tropical jungle.

"That looks nice," Brian proclaimed. "Let's check it out and see how much it is."

We drove into the complex and approached a gate. We would later learn than almost every nice complex in Florida had a gate for the entrance. We drove through and immediately noticed the cobblestone driveway. There were palm trees everywhere. It was completely mesmerizing. The air smelled fresh, like a mix between salty air and tangerines.

We pulled up to the leasing office. This place seemed to be a little different from the one before. It wasn't quite as upscale. This would be a good thing because the rent should be cheaper. Also, we didn't want to be surrounded by a bunch of uptight people.

We were greeted by a young blond-haired girl, probably a little older than we were. She was very petite and pretty, so Brian's eyes perked up immediately. He was very attracted to her type. I thought she was good-looking, but I'm more attracted to dark hair and darker skin. The complete opposite of me that's for sure.

"Hello, my name is Ashley. Are you guys looking at renting an apartment?" she asked with her *twangy* little accent.

I loved the southern accent. That alone could do it for me. "Yes," I said, "we're inquiring about a two bedroom apartment. We went down the road to Wildershire, but they were a bit too expensive for our taste."

"That's not surprising," she said, with a laugh. "They are a bit over priced, that's for sure. Well, our two bedroom apartments start at about nine hundred dollars a month. Depending on the size, they go up to twelve hundred dollars. The nine hundred dollar apartments for rent are about nine hundred and fifty square feet."

I thought that didn't sound too bad.

"Sounds much better to me," Brian stated. "That would only be about four hundred and fifty each."

"Do you want me to show you gentleman around?" she asked.

"Yes that would be nice," Brian said. He looked like a sixth grader seeing boobs for the first time.

It only took about ten minutes for us to decide this is what we wanted. She'd showed us a beautiful little condo. It was small, but spacious enough for us.

"This'll do," Brian said, knowing damn well this little hot number could show him about anything and he'd like it.

Everything looked good to me. We also loved the location. "Let's do it."

We moved all of our stuff into our apartment. We both wanted the master bedroom so we decided to play *rock, paper, scissors* for it. Just one round. Much to the dismay of Brian, I won the battle, and won the rights to the master bedroom.

It took us about two hours to unload everything into the apartment. It was colder that night, but forty-five degrees is still better than fifteen degrees. Brian and I were wearing shorts and t-shirts. I'm sure we looked funny to a few of our neighbors that we met that night. They were garbed up with sweaters, sweatshirts, jackets and jeans.

We didn't care. We were happy to be out of the snow. By midnight, all our stuff was moved into the apartment. What an exhausting day. We had been up since seven a.m. making this whole process happen. We put on a movie— *Dumb and Dumber* with Jim Carrey and Jeff Daniels was our choice. It was probably at least the hundredth time I had seen it. Brian grabbed a couple of Bud Lights from the fridge and we toasted to our new home.

Chapter Fourteen
The Weather

The wintertime in Florida is absolutely perfect. It doesn't rain very much. The luminance of the bright sunlight seemed to be at maximum potential on most days. The skies were as blue as an ocean. We had a nice little pond behind our apartment and a gorgeous collection of palm trees cascaded in the breeze just a few feet from it. You could smell the fresh green leaves and the pungent smell of the orange trees surrounding our apartment. It's as if we had died and gone to heaven. Floridians get a kick out of it, but I think that sometimes they take the great weather for granted. Unless you have spent several winters up north, it's hard to really get a clue about how depressing it can be.

I could get used to this. For a while, it was fun to call home and talk to my family and friends. "How is the weather?" they would ask.

"Absolutely perfect," I would say, almost bragging. "It sure beats the hell out of a Michigan Winter." I had been down to Florida in the wintertime before, but the realization of this becoming a permanent thing had me smiling from ear and ear.

Brian and I decided not to worry about jobs for at least a couple weeks. I had friends in Orlando and they wanted to come over and hang out with us in our new humble abode. We took them out on the town for dinner and drinks, and then subsequently spent the next few days lying around hung-over.

The next couple of weeks felt like spring break. As if we were still on an extended vacation. My brother and his buddies came down from Kalamazoo College in Michigan to spend spring break with us. It was a hell of a time.

We took them to watch a few spring training games. Our beloved Detroit Tigers play their spring ball in nearby Lakeland, which is only a half-hour drive away. It was also where my Grandpa and Grandma Krohn once had a house. It's crazy because I didn't realize how close it was to where I lived.

We took them to the beaches as well. If you haven't been to a beach in Florida, I highly recommend it. It's much different from going to Lake Michigan or to a beach up north. And you can pretty much go anytime of the year.

We took them to Siesta Key beach in Sarasota. Siesta Key beach was perennially ranked in the top ten beaches in the United States. The sand is white and powdery soft and the water is gorgeous with breathtaking scenery. It is most definitely well deserved as being one of the best in the country that's for sure.

Damon and the boys wanted to hit up some bars and nightclubs. They had all recently turned twenty-one so they were itching for the bar scene. Tampa has a pretty solid nightlife—nothing like Chicago or other huge cities, but it was definitely more lively than Kalamazoo's.

Despite the difference in weather, scenery, bars and nightlife, there was an even more distinct difference in something. The answer? Women. A huge difference. Okay, so there are a lot of beautiful women in Michigan— all shapes and sizes, you know the deal—but here there was a plethora of beautiful girls everywhere we went, and the biggest difference was diversity. There was an abundance of beautiful Spanish women, Asian woman, black women and of course white women.

I simply wasn't used to the diversity, and I loved it. Growing up in Hillsdale County, to say there was a lack of diversity would be an understatement. Kalamazoo didn't have hardly any Spanish women either. Certainly, it was more diverse than Jonesville, but seeing this many beautiful Spanish women was very pleasing to me.

A couple months prior to moving down to Florida, I jokingly told my family I was going to meet my wife sometime soon after I moved down. We were having drinks at my aunt's house on Christmas Eve and I announced to everybody that I would find my wife and she would be a Latina. That is what I was most attracted to and that's what I wanted.

After Damon and his boys went back to Michigan, we only had a few days before Brian's family would be coming down. People love it when they have someone close to them that lives in Florida. Who could blame them? It gives them a chance to escape the cold.

We had a great time with his family as well. The same routine applied as we took them to the beach and to various restaurants in the area. Being so close to the ocean, there is an abundance of seafood restaurants down here. If you are a lover of crab, fish, lobster and other seafood entrees, you will find that Florida and the Tampa Bay area has a wealth of great seafood restaurants to from which to choose.

Two more weeks had gone by and people finally stopped visiting. I love to have visitors, but it was nice to be free of obligation for a change. We had officially lived in Florida for two months. It was quite comical because it still felt like we were on vacation. The weather in March and April was marvelous. It was perpetually sunny, in the range of seventy-five to eighty-three degrees every day, with rarely any rain. We spent a lot of time laying at the pool by day and sitting in the hot tub at night. We had drinks occasionally. We even received a letter from the front office asking us to remember to throw away our beer cans.

I had been looking for jobs via Monster and CareerBuilder. Most of the jobs were related to sales and marketing positions. I would try that if I had to, but I wasn't too keen on it. My degree in psychology had its limitations and I knew it. It was hard enough to find a job anywhere.

Brian got a call from a construction company, which was good news. Considering his degree was in construction management, we thought he had a very solid chance of landing the position.

Several more days went by. Running, working out and playing basketball consumed a lot of my time. I was really getting into shape. I had moved down to Florida weighing in at about one hundred and seventy pounds. I was already down to one hundred and sixty and it had only been two months. I was almost the same weight I was when I graduated high school. What little *six-pack* I had in my abdominal muscles before, had started to show again.

There were a lot of younger people that lived in our little community. The basketball court was full almost every night. We would play your typical five-on-five basketball. Only ten people could play at once, so there were always a few guys that had to wait their turn.

I could still shoot it with the best of them. We played by ones and twos. I would hit a barrage of three pointers before the other team even realized what hit them. *If only I could have taken this many shots in high school, I could have been all-state and averaged thirty points a game.* Oh well. Deep down, I was more comfortable being the unsung hero anyway. Although it was fun to be the go-to guy once in awhile. Regardless of any awards or accolades, our team was phenomenal in high school and I wasn't the only great player. Not by any means. On any given night, any one of our starters could be the man.

Now I just played with a bunch of washed-up dudes and *baller wannabees*. It got to the point where everybody in the gym wanted the white boy with Abercrombie shorts and the surfer boy hair to be on their team. It felt pretty good. Overall, it was fun to play ball again and it took up a lot of my time in the evenings.

Brian finally got a call back from the construction company. He got the job and would start that next Monday. He was assigned a position as assistant superintendent of a job site. I was happy for him, but it made me realize that I needed to get a job myself.

About a week after Brian's hiring, I too had an interview. It was with a company in Largo, Florida. Largo was about fifty minutes away and the job involved social work. I wasn't too keen on the position, but really felt some pressure to get a job, finally. It wasn't even a money issue. The fact was I felt a little guilty since Brian had started to work. My day-to-day operations of working out, playing ball and just hanging out became a little banal.

Being a psychology major, social work was a job suitable for someone like me, and some of the work I did in Michigan had helped to prepare me for this position. As usual, I nailed the interview in impeccable fashion. They absolutely loved me. The fact that I was a male helped me out as well. Social work jobs are filled predominantly by women. After the interview took place with the head of operations, my supervisor introduced herself and it was evident she liked what she saw. She could tell I genuinely cared about helping others in need.

I had a three-week training that I needed to attend at the University of South Florida. I didn't mind this because it was only a twenty-minute drive.

Brian and I were both working and it was nice to have a routine going. Instead of hanging out all the time, we saw each other in the evenings and really only went out on the weekends.

It can be easy to get sick of someone—even though he was one of my best friends, we started to get on each other's nerves. Our little peccadilloes, which were once hysterical to each other, started to wear off. When you're primarily around one person, and one person only, after awhile things get a little monotonous. We had essentially been inseparable since December and six months of seeing someone every day was starting to wear on me.

Chapter Fifteen
Trouble in Paradise

It was now the beginning of May. Brian and I had officially lived in Florida for three months. Things were going great until one evening Brian stormed into the apartment and proceeded to slam the door shut.

"I've been laid off," Brian bellowed emphatically. "I got to work today and those bastards told me they needed to make some cuts. They needed to get rid of a bunch of people I guess. Those assholes just let me go, right on the spot."

"Holy shit, man." I said. "I can't believe they would just drop you like that. What a bunch of bitches."

"What the hell am I going to do now?" Brian yelled. "I'm running out of money. I don't know if I can afford to live down here anymore."

"That really sucks," I said, as I breathed out a long sigh. "Maybe you should fly back to Michigan and be with your family for a little bit. Feel things out for a while."

"Yeah I need to figure something out," Brian replied in a negative tone. "I want a job in construction and I'll take it wherever I can. If it's in Michigan, then it's in Michigan."

"I support your decision, whatever it may be," I said. "If you want to move back to Michigan, go ahead. You got to do what suits you best."

Three more days went by and it was now the weekend. My social work job was going okay. I was in Largo, finally. It was a long drive, but a job is a job.

Brian was flying back to Michigan in the morning. He had told his parents he needed to come back and try to find a job up there. He wasn't giving up on Florida though. He put in some applications to various other construction companies in the area.

As I drove Brian to the airport that morning, I was a little relieved. Even though I loved living with Brian, I felt like we needed a little break anyway. Hopefully he would find a permanent job that would ultimately make him happy. Maybe it was in Michigan.

I got back home that afternoon and turned on the TV. The benefits of being alone consisted of watching whatever I wanted and doing whatever I wanted. I got on the computer and just surfed the net aimlessly. We still had a few Coronas left from the night before so I sipped on one and just reflected on the last few months.

It was nice to be working down here. My job didn't pay much, but it could have been worse. I relished my weekends because it was time to gain my peace of mind back.

It was May 15 and I was finally starting to get into the scheme of things at my job. As a social worker, I felt immense pressure always to be on my A-game. My daily tasks consisted of lots of paperwork followed by family visits in the late afternoon and evenings. It was then that I saw a true glimpse of struggle.

Growing up middle class, I hadn't been exposed to financial hardships, not like this. When I into some of these homes, I saw a world that I had not been accustomed to. I didn't know what it was like to live in a one-bedroom apartment with eight people. Such was the case, when I frequented the south side in St. Petersburg. Most of these apartment complexes were so worn down, it would take me a half hour to find the right number. I was always a little nervous walking up to the door. You never really knew what you were going to see.

On this one particular occasion, I walked into the home of a young African-American couple. They were a little bit older than I was. They were a little apprehensive to let me into their home and to start talking to me. Nevertheless, they were on my caseload and I was there to check on their kids and make sure everything was okay.

Even though my appearance was much different from theirs, they seemed to relate to me. Not because I was in the same situation as them. It was because I had an innate ability to develop instant rapport with someone. Within thirty seconds of introductions, I noticed one of their little kids had a Detroit Pistons shirt on.

"Hey, I like the shirt, buddy," I said genuinely to the little boy lying on the couch. "I'm from Michigan so the Pistons are my favorite team." Considering their child had a Pistons shirt, most likely they were from Michigan as well.

"Yeah," the woman said as she smiled, "we moved down from Detroit a few years ago. We still love our Detroit Pistons no matter what though."

"That's awesome," I said. "I'm from Kalamazoo. I went to Western Michigan."

"Over on the west side of the state, right?" the guy asked?

"Yeah, that's right," I replied. "About a half hour from Lake Michigan. We're pretty much right in the middle of Chicago and Detroit."

Although, I was supremely proud of growing up in Jonesville, I never told anybody that is where I was originally from. This was only because hardly anybody else had heard of it. Unless you were from Hillsdale County or a county nearby, you wouldn't have a clue where it was.

As we made conservation, I couldn't help but look around at my surroundings. There was no judgment in me, but as I walked around and took a gander at the living situation, I couldn't help but feel sorry for them. It was appalling and unfortunate at the same time. It wasn't really their fault. They were doing the best with what they had.

The young couple had two little kids, aged four and two. Also, they had adopted a niece and a nephew who were around the same age. Apparently, the man's sister was a single mother and had recently been arrested for drugs. The kids needed somewhere to go, so they took them in. This young couple told me they couldn't bear the thought of the little ones going into the system. Going into the system means your children are taken into custody by Child Protective Services because you couldn't adequately care for them.

This was essentially what we did. This was my job. My job consisted of analyzing a family's situation and trying to decide if the children were safe. This was a big responsibility. Our jobs were very impactful in the whole dynamics of the families we visited.

If the situation was at least halfway ideal and the kids were safe in a nice, clean and friendly environment, we were good to go. However, if the home looked like a catastrophe, then we had a problem. Unfortunately, this particular place was very messy. Dishes were piled up as if they hadn't been washed in days. The bedroom looked like a hurricane went through it. And last but not least, there were six people living in this one bedroom apartment. Two of the children slept in the room with the couple, and the other two slept on the pullout couch in the living room.

The couple were struggling to find jobs. While these unfortunate circumstances were something I could sympathize with, it was my job to report it. Nobody says you have to live like kings, but the kids weren't exactly being raised the way they should.

This is where the predicament with my job started. I wanted to do the right thing. It was imperative that I kept the children's best interests as the main factor in making a decision. This couple seemed nice, but maybe taking on two more kids in their situation wasn't the best idea.

I told my supervisor about the situation. She told me that kids get taken away from families all the time. Still, in my heart, it just didn't seem right for me to make that decision. She went with me that very next week to visit the same particular couple.

We walked into the apartment and it seemed to be in worse shape than it was before. There were several empty beer cans just sitting on the kitchen table. Not only that, but the place reeked of marijuana smoke. The two-year-old girl had a diaper on that smelled as if it hadn't been changed in two days—the whole place smelled awful.

My supervisor took one look at me and I knew what needed to be done. I called Child Protective Services and they would be on their way in the next hour. We explained to the young couple why we made the call. This place was not suitable for children to live in.

"How in the hell are you going to tell me this place ain't suitable?" the mother yelled at the top of her lungs. "I thought you liked us. Get the fuck out of my house now."

"Ma'am, we're just going our jobs." My supervisor's words cut deeply into their wounds. "This place is a disaster zone and this is a dangerous environment for children."

Then we decided it would be better to go outside and wait in the parking lot. We had to make sure they weren't going to try to take off.

Approximately thirty minutes later, Child Protective Services finally showed up. They spent a few minutes going over our paperwork and proceeded to walk into the apartment. We stayed in the parking lot. A whirlwind of emotions ran through me over the next few minutes. I knew we were doing the right thing, but at what cost? I knew the kids deserved better than that. However, I didn't like the uneasy feeling of what had transpired over the last hour.

It's hard to forget the pain I observed in that mother's eyes that day. I have never been precisely in her shoes, but I knew what it was like to say goodbye to someone that I loved. At least, they would have the opportunity to get their kids back. Some of us can only hope to be so lucky.

My supervisor kept reminding me that we did the right thing. The couple were not currently providing a suitable environment for their children. They needed to get jobs, stop using drugs and prove to the state they were responsible enough to take care of their children.

Chapter Sixteen
First Anniversary Alone

Over the course of that next weekend, I sat alone on my couch. Brian was still up in Michigan. I just sat there, drinking a corona and pondering life as I knew it. *Man, this was hard as hell.*

I kept telling myself that we did the right thing. I started contemplating my existence within this company. I simply didn't know if I was cut out for social work. I wanted to make a positive impact on peoples' lives, but it was extremely difficult to think positive because this job was taking a toll on me. Maybe I wasn't in the right frame of mind to be doing this. To make matters worse, it was almost May 16—the date my mom passed away—the anniversary is always very hard on me.

Something was very different this time though—I was alone. I had spent the first three years under the umbrella of loved ones. I spent the first one with my girlfriend and she helped me through it. We watched a movie that year. It was nice to have a shoulder to cry on.

The next couple years on May 16, I hung out with Damon and a few of his friends at Kalamazoo College. Being around a bunch of people keeps your mind occupied. When you're busy, it's easier to hide the feelings of sadness and despair.

This was really tough—a lot tougher than I thought it would be. Being alone sucks during a time of need. This was nobody's fault but mine. I was the one who left Michigan. I was the one who left my family. I would just have to be strong and deal with this on my own.

Most likely, I would just stay home, pound some beers and watch a movie. I didn't feel like going out. I had met a few friends at work that I got along with, but I didn't feel like hanging out with them this weekend. They had invited me to see a Tampa Bay Rays baseball game. I had gone to a couple with them already, yet this time I didn't feel like it.

After I pounded about six coronas, I decided to break out the Southern Comfort that hid in the freezer. *Ah. The good stuff.* This would surely take my pain away. I took a shot of *SoCo* and it went down nice and smooth. I would have another one and chase it down with another Corona.

I was feeling good and lit at this time. I would surely be hung-over the next day, but I didn't care. All I cared about was getting rid of these lonely feelings.

I made a call to my best friend in the world. Sam always seemed to be there when I called. He was going through his own trials and tribulations during this time so we could definitely relate to each other. Our problems stemmed from different things, yet we were always able to empathize with each other.

"What's up, playa?" I said with a noticeable slur in my speech. "What the hell are you doing?"

"Sitting around watching a movie, having a few beers," he responded with laughter in his voice. "What else would I be doing on a Saturday night? You know how I roll."

"True that, son. I've been pounding a few myself. I just took a couple shots of *SoCo* so I'm starting to get pretty drunk."

"Hell yeah," he said. "Nothing wrong with that."

"Do you know what tomorrow is, Sam?"

"Umm...what is tomorrow?" he asked. "May

113

sixteenth? Oh yeah. I do. Sorry, man. I know it's a really tough day for you."

"Yeah it is. Sorry to blab on and bring it up. But usually I'm hanging with my family, or you guys, so it sort of takes my mind off of things."

"I know it's going to be a hard day, but you'll pull through it. You're strong."

Not as strong as you think, I thought.

"I might have to give you a call tomorrow and talk for a bit. Although, I will be pretty hung-over so I might just sleep most of the damn day."

"Give me a call anytime you want, dude," he said. "I'm working tomorrow night and will have my phone on me."

"Thanks. Well, I'm going to let you go. I got a couple more beers to drink before I pass out."

"I will be doing the same," he said.

"One."

"One."

Sam and I always say "one" instead of saying goodbye. We saw it on one of our favorite movies. In the movie *Belly*, Nas and DMX always said it to each other to end their conversation. We loved it and decided to use it for the hell of it. I guess our inner thug was revealing itself.

I drank a couple more beers and passed out.

I woke up the next morning feeling like crap. I felt anxious, nervous, shaky and nauseous—you name it. I had immediately regretted my decision to get drunk the night before. Not a smart move. At least it was Sunday. The only problem was I would most likely be depressed all day. In addition, I would also most likely be hung-over the next day for work.

It was going to be an odd day—the first time I had ever spent the anniversary of my mother's death alone. Some people may actually prefer to be alone on a day like this, but not me. I didn't really like to be alone.

I had a copy of Mom's journal entries. Taryn had the originals. One day I borrowed them and made myself a few copies as a keepsake. They are cool to look at once in a while. They provide a lot of great insight into our lives. A lot of the stuff she shared about us back then is still true to this day. I happened to look at them that day and one of the entries stated the same thing. It reads, "Ryan loves to be around people. He likes to make conversation with people and just hang out. He doesn't really like to be alone. Especially at night. He is one of those older brothers that actually likes to share a room with his younger brother."

It was such a hindrance feeling like this. I wished I had a Xanax or something. Giving in and taking something would have been a complete anomaly for me, but it would have been nice to have something to calm my nerves.

Three hours passed and I still felt shaky. I didn't talk to anyone that day. Sam had actually called me in the afternoon to check on me. I'm glad he called but I didn't feel like talking to anyone, so I didn't answer. I didn't even feel like eating, but I managed to scarf down a sandwich later that evening.

I spent the last few hours of the day just watching TV. I thought watching something funny would cheer me up, so I put *Dumb and Dumber* in the DVD player. It helped a little bit. But I couldn't help but think of my mom most of the day. I missed her so much. Next year would be different.

Chapter Seventeen
Maintaining the Status Quo

As the summer hit, I was still surviving my job as a social worker. Although I wasn't happy with it anymore, I was just keeping it for the hell of it. Brian was back and forth between Michigan and Florida. He was doing odd jobs in both areas, but he had concluded that he would be moving back to Michigan at the end of the summer. It would be sad to see him go. However, I supported his decision wholeheartedly. It presented an interesting predicament, as I most definitely couldn't afford this place on my own. Luckily, we just had a month-to-month lease so I could break it at anytime. This would offer another problem for me though. I was going to have to find another place to live and I wasn't ready to give up on Florida.

I was definitely not used to this level of heat and humidity. Michigan never got this humid in the summer. And it never goes away. For five months of the year, it will never dip below eighty-five degrees. It doesn't matter what time of the day it is—it could be three o'clock in the morning and it would still be hot and muggy out. No matter where you go or what you do you will sweat. And I was already a hot-blooded person. I get hot very easy and I'm quick to sweat.

I had been out west to Arizona and Las Vegas in the summertime. The dry heat out there can lead to hotter temperatures, yet I never sweated so much in my life as I did down in Florida. I love the warm winters and the subtropical climate, but sometimes it gets to the point where enough is enough.

That first summer, I even debated if a hot, humid summer could actually be worse than a frigid Michigan winter. Even though some people would say the latter is better, I still wasn't buying it. I wasn't too fond of constantly sweating profusely. However, as many Floridians would tell me, that was what pools and air conditioning were for.

Even though I did my fair share of bitching and complaining, I would have to admit that a hot summer still beat the cold. There is no escaping the bone-chilling cold and gloomy skies of a Michigan winter. I'm talking so *fricken* cold, it feels like your fingers and toes could just fall off. You can take a deep breath and it feels like someone punched you in the chest.

Now after spending a few summers in Florida, I am finally used to it. I'll go home occasionally for Christmas or Thanksgiving and that's it. People can come down to see me. Unless it's a holiday or some mandatory visit I have to make, you won't see me up there.

I was essentially alone for the majority of the summer. Regardless of the weather, I was still plugging away at my job, even though it was still hard and I saw some more crazy stuff.

I encountered all types of people from different walks of life. In one day, I would come across two polar opposites on the financial spectrum of things. In the morning, I could meet with an affluent couple living ocean-side in a mansion on Clearwater Beach. One particular couple served host to about a dozen boys in their home. The home was massive as it must have been around five thousand square feet. Without a doubt, one of the biggest homes I had ever set foot in.

The boys ranged from middle school to high school. They each bunked up with one other boy. They all slept in large bedrooms with computers, TVs and more video games than you can count. When the boys got bored with their *toys*, they could entertain themselves by swimming in the indoor pool that was attached to the mansion. Or if they were real lucky, their foster father would take them on the ocean for a boat ride.

The boys had a great life at this home. The foster parents made a great living. They owned several Subways in the area and the cash was rolling in. It should also be noted they received a nice chunk of change from the state for housing each boy.

Overall, they did a fantastic job providing a loving home for those boys. I loved these cases. They were the easy ones.

On the other spectrum of things, I also had the fine privilege of visiting the "ghetto" in south St. Pete. These were usually bad situations. They were typically similar to the situation that haunted me from just a few weeks prior. We were forced to intervene many times because the family didn't provide a stable home. While I appreciated their struggle and adversity, the children's best interests must always be the focal point.

Taking a child away from an unfit parent was the right thing to do, but it caused a lot of wear and tear on me.

Chapter Eighteen
Decisions

The month of July was a very lonely time for me. Brian wasn't around. He was up in Michigan finalizing his new job at a construction site and my days just seemed to all be the same. I was going to a job I didn't like. Everybody annoyed the hell out of me and I was so damn irritable most of the time.

I was supposed to be happy down here. What the hell was going on? I had started to get this anxious feeling in the pit of my stomach every morning when I woke up. It was a terrible feeling. I felt lonely and depressed.

This wasn't the way it was supposed to be. I just wasn't doing what I wanted to do in life. So that begged the million-dollar question—what did I want to do. I didn't have the answer and it ate me up inside.

I knew that I didn't want to go to graduate school anymore. I knew that I didn't want to live in Michigan. But being puzzled about the rest just boggled up my confused mind even more. One of the main dilemmas I encountered was that I wanted to do something special. I wanted to make a huge difference in this world. Not that what I was doing wasn't important, I knew I was making a positive impact on the lives of children I visited. Because of me, there were children out there living a happier life. I took kids out of crappy situations and put them into better ones. This was a very positive thing. The only problem is the positives weren't outweighing the negatives. I was making a difference, but I needed something more. I

119

needed to figure that out.

For some social workers, I'm sure it was enough, but for me it wasn't. I needed to reach people on a different level, a higher plane. Maybe it was arrogance. Maybe I felt a sense of entitlement. I didn't look down on social workers though. I didn't care what people said about the measly salary. I ignored the comments I received from stuck up girls at various bars in South Tampa—that infamous conversation anybody in my shoes has reluctantly had.

"So what do you do for a living?" they would ask.

"Well, I'm a social worker. I help out kids that are in need."

"Aw, that's so sweet," I would hear. "That is very noble of you, but how do you pay all your bills?"

"Well I don't make very much so it's pretty difficult," I would respond awkwardly.

What did I expect at a bar though? Half of the women were looking for a sugar-daddy that drove a Benz and worked as an investment banker downtown.

My family and I had been a close unit my entire life. After my mom's passing, I became even closer with my dad, Taryn and Damon. They offered a shoulder to lean on, but we were all a part of this terrible tragedy. All of us had lost the number one person in our life. We persevered around and through each other. Taryn and Damon kept me going and vice versa.

Before, it was so much easier because they were only a short drive away. Having them in the same city as me was a huge advantage. It was also a blessing as we were able to meet frequently to discuss life and how things were going. Now all I could do was talk on the phone. That damn phone. I was so depressed on the weekends that I would just walk and walk—all around my complex and I would talk mostly just to Sam or Travis. I would tell them how I was feeling and about my problems at work.

I spoke to my family every couple of weeks too. It was harder to talk to Taryn and Damon simply because they were extremely busy with their respective studies. Damon was at Kalamazoo College studying psychology and playing on the basketball team. Taryn was busy working on her master's degree. I didn't want to bother them and I didn't want to talk about the things that were bothering me. I didn't want to worry them. They had enough on their plates. So, I acted as if everything was fine when I did talk to them.

I was now seeing a girl and we got along pretty well, so I told them about my relationship and how it was progressing. She and I were hanging out on a nightly basis after awhile. We fell for each other pretty hard, right off the bat. I wasn't really looking for a girlfriend, but it just happened. I think we both needed somebody at that stage in our lives.

Chapter Nineteen
Sinking Deeper

Fuck this depression sucks. I was so goddammed sick of it, I couldn't even think straight. When I say I couldn't think straight, I mean it literally too. My anxiety and depressive thoughts had started to consume me. I felt lightheaded and dizzy half of the time. It felt like I was strung out on drugs or something. But the fact was I remained stone-cold sober for the most part. I only drank occasionally, because I knew it would only prolong my feelings of anxiety.

Sometimes I wanted to punch someone in the face, but I couldn't. Another rainy day. They say a Michigan winter can be depressing. Well how about a Florida summer that darkens up like clockwork around five p.m. every day? It then looks like the whole atmosphere has been engulfed by a black hole, followed by the heaviest rain you'll ever see.

It really sucks to drive in it. You can't see anything two feet in front of you when it downpours. Every day when I left work it rained. My already long and repetitious drive turned into a ninety-minute ordeal with the traffic and the rain. Sometimes, when I was having a bad day, I cried on the way home. I just couldn't help it. It could be a sad song—it's true what they say, don't listen to Coldplay when you're depressed—or maybe an accident I saw on the highway. But on the *really* bad days, my eyes would just well up for no reason. On those days, it felt like a dark cloud followed me around as if I was in a *Charlie Brown* cartoon. It felt like it was grabbing onto my body and trying to take over my whole existence.

I left work each day at five o'clock and I never got home until six thirty. By the time I grabbed dinner, it was already seven. Half of the time, I didn't have enough time to work out. On the days that I did, I was too exhausted to muster a good workout anyway.

The fact of the matter was I didn't need a workout to feel sore—my whole body hurt most of the time. My legs were sore. My arms were sore. My neck, back and chest all hurt too. What in the hell was happening? I was only twenty-five years old. I shouldn't feel like this.

Seriously, my body felt like I had just boxed twelve rounds with Mike Tyson in his prime. I was too young to feel like this. It would be different if I had put my body through a series of intense workouts that warranted the excruciating pain. But I wasn't doing that.

In actuality, it was the anxiety and depression causing the pain in my body. It took me awhile to realize this. So not only does this affect mood, thinking and rationalization skills, but it affects the body too. My anxiety got so bad it was even affecting my work. I could no longer tolerate foolishness. It really hampered my focus and concentration. I couldn't focus on anything for more than ten minutes. It was extremely difficult getting all my weekly tasks finished.

At the start of the week, we made individual checklists of about thirty things we needed to do for the week. It would take me all week to complete my checklist, but by Friday afternoon, I would be done. When Friday afternoon rolled up, I felt content I didn't have to worry about anything over the weekend.

After I completed my list, I would go back to my office and start to fret about what needed to be done for the next week. As the anxiety intensified, it became increasingly difficult to start my list, let alone finish it. When lunchtime came, I had typically wasted a couple hours just trying to figure out what I needed to do and in what order it needed to be done.

I knew that I needed to go visit a few homes and that started to bother me. Thinking about these visits and what I knew I would see stressed me out. Before, I could easily deal with it. Seeing filthy homes and shitty living situations just became second nature to me. After a couple months, I just grew immune to it. However, the misfortunes of these people started to take a toll on me. It's not as if I could do anything about it either. Most of these people struggled financially. What was I supposed to do? Give them a bunch of money? I couldn't do that.

It developed into a combination of things. I was lonely because I wasn't hanging out with family or friends—everybody was in Michigan and I hadn't really met anybody here that I really clicked with yet.

I felt isolated on the weekends because all anybody wanted to do was party and just get hammered. While I liked to go out on occasion and do the same, I just got sick of it. Being hung-over and tired was hard on my health, both my mental and physical health. But on the weekends that I did go out and party, I would always go all out.

Friday evenings started off with ten-dollar- all-you-can-drink happy-hour. That was anything, except for shots. Beer and mixed drinks were limitless for two hours. It was a free-for-all. My co-workers and I had very stressful weeks and then it was time to let the alcohol take out all our frustrations.

This was just the beginning of the night though. We would usually stay there for a few hours and then hit up a few more spots. Before we knew it, it was closing time and we were cabbing it home or staying at someone's house nearby. Those nights were fun while they lasted. The only problem is, I went so hard on those nights that I'd literally be hung-over and virtually worthless for three whole days. It inevitably hampered my Monday mornings, and the way things were going it affected Tuesday and Wednesday too.

I learned my lesson after doing that a few times, so as long as I was working, I couldn't do it anymore. I knew that something needed to give. I couldn't keep on living this anxious and depressed life. I hated the feeling of loneliness.

I'm a personable and charismatic guy, so perhaps I should have gone out more and made some friends. That would have been a viable option, but I just didn't feel like it. I needed to see someone familiar. I needed to *feel* something familiar. When I left Michigan, I left all of my family and best friends. Something needed to change for the better or else I would be moving back. I didn't want to move back. I made this huge decision to move here and I didn't want to feel like a failure by moving back after only six months. After all, I was supposed to be happy down here and nobody knew how I truly felt. With the exception of a one or two people, everyone thought I was having the time of my life in Florida.

Chapter Twenty
Best Friends

Some great news finally came. Danny was moving down to Florida. I couldn't believe it. Brian was moving out in August and Danny would take his spot. The timing couldn't have been more perfect.

A few months back, Brian and I were both in Kalamazoo talking to Danny about moving to Tampa. He said he really wanted to join us down here in the Sunshine State. To be honest, I didn't think he would follow through with it. Like us, he had a ton of family and friends in Michigan and I didn't think he would come. Nothing against Brian, but I certainly gelled a little better with Danny. It seems like we had more in common, plus he was my first best friend in Kalamazoo.

Danny had just completed his student teaching at a middle school in Portage. He'd had an interview with a high school in Florida and he had landed the job on the spot. It was at Ridge Community High School in Davenport, Florida—almost an hour away. The school was closer to Orlando than our apartment, but he didn't care. He wanted a teaching job and he got it.

Although he wanted to teach American History of some sorts, a job in ESE would suffice for the moment— ESE stands for Exceptional Student Education. Danny's job would consist of co-teaching with a regular education teacher. His primary responsibility was to help teach the various students with disabilities. These disabilities could range from Attention Deficit Disorder to Asperger's syndrome.

Each ESE student has an IEP, or Individual Education Plan, which is a written, legal document that includes each student's specific accommodations and modifications to ensure success. For many students, once classified as being an ESE student, they could still participate in a regular classroom as long as an ESE teacher was present in the classroom as well.

This would be a perfect job for Danny. He had a heart of gold and he was one of the least judgmental people I have ever met. He had worked with troubled youth in Kalamazoo for years. He was energetic as hell and loved a challenge.

At the end of August, Danny was now in the process of moving into our apartment. Brian had left the week before so Danny took his old room. That was the good news. The bad news was that I still hated my job and I just couldn't deal with it anymore. While I have never been to jail, it got to the point where it felt like a prison sentence to me. My anxiety and depression were still present, still affecting my work, but I managed to get everything done for the most part. I still hated to see underprivileged families suffer the way they did.

I had contemplated going to a doctor to try and obtain a prescription for Xanax, but I didn't. I just wasn't fond of taking pills. I didn't even like to take painkillers for a headache. I just suffered with the pain. Having Danny move in produced some happiness and that helped.

One night shortly after Danny had moved in, I told him I was quitting. "I can't do it anymore," I announced. "It's kind of weird and shitty at the same time, but I'm done." For some reason, I felt nervous as the words came out, but I knew he would support my decision.

"Really?" he asked. "Damn, I didn't realize you were

unhappy there."

I proceeded to confide to Danny about how I was feeling. I told him about the various homes I visited, how it took a toll on me, and that I just couldn't do it anymore.

"That's understandable. You got to do what makes you happy. Wait...you're not moving back now are you?" Danny became worried for a split second.

"Naw, man, don't worry about that. I'm staying right here."

Even though I had my troubles in the Sunshine State, I had decided awhile ago that I wouldn't give up and bail. I was definitely going to give it some more time. I deserved it. Danny deserved it.

"Okay, good deal," he said relieved. "I thought you might decide to move back, like Brian. You gotta do what you gotta do, but considering I just moved down, I figured you would at least stay for a little while."

We enjoyed a laugh for a few seconds.

"Yeah, no shit. By the way, I know you just moved in and all, but now I'm moving back to Michigan. Have a good life." I said with a facetious tone.

Danny started to crack up. We always had a way of making each other laugh during awkward situations.

"I may quit my job, but I could never quit you, big boy," I added, laughing the whole time.

"I'm here for a while. I moved down here for a reason. I just have to find it."

"So what's the plan now?" he asked.

"Well I just put in my two-weeks this morning. So I have fourteen more days in hell and then I'll probably relax for a week or two, try to figure things out. I know I don't want to do sales again. I don't want to work with mortgages or anything. I tried social work and didn't like it. Maybe I'll try and work as a male stripper or something."

Danny was still laughing. He knew I liked to joke around a lot. Looking back, hell, maybe I should have tried stand-up. I could have gone on stage and performed for amateur night. You never know. Perhaps, I could have made it on Leno and made a career out of it. I guess I'll never know.

Ryan Krohn

Chapter Twenty-One
The Student Becomes the Teacher

Although the commute was long, Danny enjoyed his new teaching position. He had to wake up between five and five thirty a.m. just to make it to the school on time, but he was a morning person, so it wasn't a big deal. He always seemed to have extra energy. I didn't know where it came from half the time. I called him the energizer bunny. He could work all day, come home, workout and still look more energized than most people who'd had the day off.

Then, one random night we had a discussion that changed me forever.

Danny suggested that I apply for a teaching job at his school. I had actually thought of it, but I had doubted that I would get hired. In the state of Florida, you don't actually need to have a degree in education to be hired as a teacher. You can have a degree in something else and still potentially get any teaching position you desire. However, you need to complete the necessary steps in order to receive your permanent teaching certificate.

The state puts you in what is known as an ACP program. ACP stands for Alternative Certification Program. It consists of a series of tests and classes you have to take in order to graduate from the program. Having met all the requirements, one could gain permanent status and then apply for a permanent teaching certificate.

"I'm telling you, bro," Danny said with excitement,

"you have a degree in psychology, plus you did social work. Are you kidding me? The school would love to have you as an ESE teacher."

"Man, I think you could be right. Hell, with my background and expertise I think I could possibly be a great match for the school."

"I can put in a good word with our department head and principal. We could be working together, how sweet would that be?"

"That could be *fricken* awesome, dude. I would hate to get up that early, but hell, that's nothing coffee can't help with."

Danny had given me a tremendous idea and I'm glad he brought it up. I was thinking about possibly going that route and him mentioning it just further promoted my self-confidence. I had thought about being a teacher from time to time. Teaching goes way back into my family history. Both my Grandpa and Grandma Krohn were teachers. And even more important, both my parents were teachers. My mom only taught for a little while before she changed to counseling, but my dad had been a teacher for over twenty years. I could be the third generation Mr. Krohn. Wow. That was pretty incredible when I really thought about it.

You don't hear stories like that often. I knew that my grandpa had made a very positive impact on the teenagers he taught, just as Dad did. When I was at Grandpa's funeral, I learned that he had been wildly loved by his students. Many of the people that attended the funeral were former students and they all spoke so highly of him. It wasn't just because he was a nice guy. It was more based on his integrity and character. He treated every student the same—it didn't matter their ethnic background, financial situation or intelligence.

They told me stories about him and all the hilarious

things he used to do. They said he was somewhat of a hard-ass and a rule-stickler, but he was highly respected because he was great at what he did. A couple guys even told me that at the time, they hated how hard he made them work, but now they were so grateful for the way he pushed them. One man, probably in his sixties, told me he had become a teacher because of my Grandpa.

My dad was looked at in the same light. He was highly respected and well liked because of the way that he treated people. Also, he was very good at making learning fun. He was a bit of a jokester at times and was exceptional at getting the students interested. He had no fear of trying new things either. He was known as the fun teacher in the school, but he didn't let kids goof off as they pleased. He simply had an uncanny ability to relate to kids, even as he got older. He would talk to them about sports, music and other things teenagers would be interested in. During a lesson, he was a master at incorporating fun things into his repertoire.

Looking back on my own high school and college days, these were definitely the kind of teachers that most appealed to me. I always remembered the great ones. To this day, I could tell you who my favorite teachers were. One of them was a teacher I had in fifth grade, but what these teachers all had in common was their unique abilities to relate to kids and make learning fun.

I wanted to be one of those teachers. I wanted to be a mentor to kids like Mom, Dad and Grandpa Krohn. When they needed to look up to someone, I wanted to be there for them.

I got an interview with the principal at Ridge Community High School. Thanks to Danny and my resume, I was asked to come in right before Christmas break.

They interview went amazing and the principal hired me as a temporary employee for an ESE position. Danny and I had never really worked together so this would be a new experience. But we were both looking forward to it.

Chapter Twenty-Two
Fresh Start

Danny and I were only at that school for one year. We both decided we needed to get a job in Hillsborough County where we lived. Danny obtained an ESE position at a middle school in Tampa and I got a job as an ESE teacher at a high school only minutes away from where we lived.

When I began teaching at East Bay, I found myself making a huge difference for the first time in awhile. I still remember that initial group of freshman that stepped into my classroom. I'm sure they were almost as nervous as I was. Here I was, a baby-faced man with no facial hair, twenty-six at the time, but I didn't look a day over nineteen, as evidenced by a few teachers yelling at me for being on my cell phone in the hallway. I couldn't help but laugh as I put the phone down, and flashed them by teacher ID.

They would smile at me, befuddled, and say, "Oh sorry, sir. I thought you were a student."

I decided I needed to grow my beard back. Whether I liked having facial hair or not, it was time. Nothing felt more awkward and embarrassing than when a fellow educator thought I was a student—at least I get a chuckle out of it now, though.

The kids looked so damn young. Did I look this young and innocent when I was a freshman? I'm sure I did. As I walked into the school, I glanced around and saw students running all over the place. I remember thinking, *holy shit, these kids look like they are ten.*

I had butterflies in my stomach and the nervousness was starting to devour me, but I thought about my mom on her first day teaching and my dad on his. I thought of my grandparents on their first days. They survived it, so why wouldn't I?

I set my emotions aside and collected myself as the students began to pour into my classroom. The bell rang to begin first period. Wow, this was it. I had my own classroom full of my very own students. I can't say I envisioned this when I was a senior in high school, I did not intend to become a teacher—it kind of just fell into my lap.

Well, it was time to properly introduce myself and give students the spiel I had been coached to give by a veteran teacher during my teacher orientation week.

"Hello, everyone. My name is Mr. Krohn." It felt strange hearing those words come out of my mouth. I was only twenty-six years old. My father was Mr. Krohn and my grandfather was Mr. Krohn. "This is my first year at East Bay High School. I previously taught in Polk County at a high school similar to this one. I am originally from a small town in Michigan and I graduated from Western Michigan University."

No one had heard of Kalamazoo or Western Michigan. When I mentioned that Derek Jeter was from Kalamazoo and Greg Jennings went to Western Michigan, I received some nods of acknowledgement. Even though I only had one semester under my belt, I couldn't let the students know that. My teaching experience was strictly on a need-to-know basis. They knew I was young, but they didn't need to know I was scared shitless too.

I talked about the accolades I had received from distinguished colleagues and how I was adept at getting students to understand the material being presented. I told them I had the respect of my former students—I really wanted to sell myself. I mentioned that even though pressure from administrators and parents was going to be intense, I remained adamant about teaching them to the best of my ability.

Later I would realize that accolades wouldn't matter if they kids weren't treated with respect. The kids didn't care where I went to college. They didn't think about things like that yet.

As the days went by, I adjusted to my surroundings and the school. I became the assistant varsity basketball coach as well as head coach for the junior varsity team. It was great to be involved in sports again. I made some great friends those first few weeks, too. Leech, Becky and Joe were all about my age, and oddly enough, all from the Midwest as well. Becky was even a fellow Western Michigan Bronco. I never knew her there, but we probably passed each other a few times on campus.

They were all experienced teachers and gave me pointers as the weeks went by. The kids came to like me quicker than I'd thought, and for the same reason students liked my dad. It was simple. They could relate to me and I didn't make any of my students feel dumb.

Considering my students all had learning disabilities, the last thing I wanted to do was make them feel dumb or inferior. They knew they were ESE. Some of the regular kids they encountered on a daily basis reminded them accordingly.

Once in a while, a kid would give up and throw his book in disgust. "I'm never going to learn this stuff, Mr. Krohn. I'm too dumb."

I reminded those students that people are smart in different ways. I'd had a friend who could barely add two plus two, but he could fix anything on a car. I knew all my times tables since I was ten years old, but I couldn't even change my oil. In addition, there are people whose IQ is off the charts, they could program a computer and do things that I could only dream of, but when it comes to dealing with people, they strike out. They couldn't teach a lesson if their life depended on it.

I told my students we need all types of workers in today's society—mechanics, custodians, construction workers, lawyers, doctors. It doesn't make you any less of person if you don't make as much money as a doctor or a lawyer. I taught them never to let anyone tell them that they were worthless or dumb. Everybody is smart in his or her own right and nobody knows everything this world has to offer.

Chapter Twenty-Three
Purpose

Oddly enough, I had many ups and downs at East Bay. *I know, right. Really? Can I find something else to bitch about?* While most of the students loved me and told me I was their favorite on a daily basis, I still had problems with certain students.

I had some that simply didn't give a crap about anything. They came to school and dozed in their seat as soon as first period began. Going in, I was naive to think all my students would want to learn. I had a small collection of students who didn't do a damn thing—and *fuck off* was a popular choice of words, by one boy in particular.

I got used to it for a while. What was I going to do? Write a referral and report him? Yeah, I tried that a few times, but he kept coming back for more. Some of these students weren't used to an adult telling them what to do, so who could blame them. They didn't have anyone at home to do it—maybe they'd never met their dad, or they barely knew their mom. So, while their moms spent most of their time working at Walmart or a gas station, they hung out at home drinking, smoking cigarettes and doing whatever they pleased.

I would try to motivate them to no avail. It took me awhile to realize that it wasn't personal. You simply can't put a gun to someone's head and make them do something. Finally, after a few more weeks of trying, I succumbed. As long as a student tried and did the work, he or she passed. The very select few who refrained from doing anything failed. It was simple as that.

I taught everything—Science, Math, Social Studies, Reading and English. It wasn't a self-contained classroom, one that consists of the same students for every period, but it was close. I had most of the same students throughout the day. There were eight periods in a day. I had one lunch and one conference period so I had six periods all to myself.

I didn't have a typical classroom full of twenty-five to thirty students. My classroom numbers ranged from six to sixteen. Sounds nice right? Most teachers can't say they only have six students in one of their classes. But considering these kids all had behavior issues and learning disabilities, it could feel like fifty kids were in the room. Some of these kids, I had as many as four times a day. Luckily, the most annoying ones and the bad apples were only once or twice—I was only tortured so much.

I was much happier at East Bay than I was at my old high school, and driving only ten miles each way was a lot better than sixty. As the months passed, I had curbed my anxiety and loneliness for the most part. Nonetheless, I still had days when I felt sad and alone. Going through a couple tumultuous relationships didn't help matters either.

You fall in love and get your heart broken—you think you're in love, but you're really not. I had experienced these types of relationships before, but the difference now was that I was in a different state of mind. Overall, I was much happier in 2007 and 2008 than I was in 2006.

That summer of 2006—I still call it *The Summer of Hell*.

It was at East Bay where I found my purpose in life. I was hired there for a reason. I just hadn't experienced it yet. I was there to be a teacher, to teach students, mold young minds and make a difference. But there was something important that I needed to accomplish, something that would make my life truly feel meaningful. I just was not one of those people that can skate through life and feel happy. I needed to make a difference. I needed something tangible and I was still trying to figure out if I belonged in Florida or not.

The spring of 2008 changed my perspective on everything. It gave me a new way to look at life. We had just finished our basketball season. My junior varsity team was okay. We had a losing record that year, but our record was better than the varsity squad's. It was in May 2008, I would find my true purpose.

On a personal level, I always dreaded the month of May. The whole month was horrible for me. Not only did the accident occur this month, but we also spent one agonizing week in a hospital, full of sadness and anguish. These awful memories still haunted me and to make matters worse, my mom died in the middle of May. And if that isn't enough, Mother's Day is always in May—the anniversary of my mom's death actually came to be on Mother's Day once. Let's just say, I got drunk as hell that day and took off work the next day.

Everybody at school was starting to get sick of being there by this time of year. Honestly, I saw it all the time with both students and teachers. Summer was approaching and that was all we could think of. We couldn't wait to get out of there and enjoy some peace and tranquility. I got to the point where I was just so exhausted. I kept on telling myself one thing—no matter what, don't call a student a name or cuss in class, no matter how far they tried to push me over the edge. Some days this was hard to do.

The special occasion that would change my life

forever happened on a Monday morning. A kid who was normally one of my best students, stormed into class and immediately put his head down on his desk. Ronnie, a freshman, was African-American and at only fourteen years of age he was one of the youngest students in my class. He was overweight and unfortunately got picked on a lot at lunchtime. I felt bad for him, but through it all he always had a smile on his face. He was always happy to see me. Teachers aren't supposed to choose favorites, but he was mine.

I approached him. "Is everything okay, Ronnie?"

Ronnie didn't say a word or even lift his head up.

"Hey, buddy, do you want to go outside and talk about it for a minute?" I had an aid for that period who could watch over the class for a few minutes while I would try and talk some sense into Ronnie.

He finally lifted his head and nodded. We walked outside of my classroom and I shut the door. "Ronnie, what's up, my man?" I asked sympathetically. "I've never seen you act like this before."

"I'm having a terrible day, Mr. Krohn," he answered with a trembling in his voice.

"Do you want to talk about it?"

"Well, I guess so, Mr. Krohn. You see today is the anniversary of my mom's death. She died on May ninth last year. I thought I could be strong today, but I should have just stayed home."

Wow. You gotta be kidding me? On this very same day, six years prior, my mom was hit by that semi-truck that ultimately changed all of our lives forever. This was craziness. And to think, I almost took the day off in self-pity.

"I'm so terribly sorry to hear that, Ronnie," I said, apologetically. "Unfortunately, I know precisely how you feel. I too know what it feels like to lose a mother. My mom was the number one person in my life and I know that your mom was invaluable to you as well."

I looked up and saw that he had tears in his eyes. I knew what I needed to do. I poked my head in the door and told my aid that Ronnie and I were going for a little walk.

We stepped outside and walked down the road. The glimmer of the sun pierced my eyes with each walking stride and the glow of the orange trees could be seen in the distance. At nine thirty in the morning, it was already in the nineties. Sweat began to form on my chest. It was hot, but I didn't care. It could have been a hundred and ten out—I needed to be outside with Ronnie. Birds chirped and the freshly mowed grass was potent as we approached a picnic table and sat down.

"We have a lot in common, Ronnie," I told him.

I explained what happened to my mom and my family six years before, how she was struck by a semi and spent a week in a coma. As I continued, Ronnie's eyes were locked on mine and I could feel his pain and suffering.

"She passed away one week later, on May sixteenth," I told him. "The year was 2002. I'll never forget it."

"Wow, Mr. Krohn," Ronnie said, as a tear rolled down his face. "I didn't know you lost your mom too."

"Yeah. It's just something I don't like to talk about, but I know exactly how you're feeling, Ronnie. And I tell you what, buddy, I went through this at twenty-one years old. You went through this at thirteen. You are strong man. I can't imagine losing my mom at thirteen. I am so proud of you and everything you have done this year. Without you and your constant positive attitude in the classroom, I may have gone insane. No matter how many times a kid disrespected me you were always there with a smile on your face."

Ronnie's tears cleared up and he smiled. "You're my favorite teacher, Mr. Krohn. Honestly, I don't know what I would do right now if you weren't here. Just having this conversation has made my day a little better."

As the words came out of Ronnie's mouth, I gritted my teeth and clenched my fists. I was trying not to cry. There is nothing wrong with crying, but I didn't want to cry like this. Not at school. Not in front of a student.

There was a ten-second pause between us, after Ronnie finished his sentence. I looked back up at him and smiled.

"This conversation has helped me too, Ronnie. You have helped me, in more ways than you know."

We walked back into my classroom just as the bell rang. The kids walked out and I sat down at my desk. I was sitting there all alone and it came to me—this was my purpose, to help kids who have experienced loss just like me. I felt elated as a boost of energy coursed its way through my body and soul. I smiled as a tear rolled down my cheek.

Chapter Twenty-Four
La Patricia Bonita

It was the winter of 2009, January 27 to be exact. It was my birthday and I was turning twenty-eight. The school year was going excellent. My junior varsity basketball team was kicking some major ass. We were on a roll, winning our last five games and our record was currently 9-3.

My dad drove down from Michigan to enjoy some vacation time out of the cold. It was cool because he made it down to watch our game on my birthday. I was a little nervous because he would be watching. We played Sarasota High School and they were good. I told the boys that not only was it my birthday, but my dad was here all the way from Michigan so they better not mess it up. They responded accordingly and the final score was 72-47. We had trounced our opposition with tenacious defense and instant offense from our best two players.

Dad and I gathered with the other coaches at Chili's and had a few celebratory beers. My dad had coached too and he said I did a good job, but he still offered some advice. He said that I needed to come up with some better out-of-bounds plays. The whole crew started laughing hard.

After about a week, my dad asked me if I had ever given Match.com a try. I answered an emphatic no, and started to laugh.

He didn't seem to think it was that funny. "I'm telling

you it works." Apparently, one of his lawyer buddies had tried it and met the women of his dreams. "I wanna try it," he said. "Sign me up for it."

"Okay, you might as well give it a whirl."

Although my dad is extremely intelligent, he has no clue how to do anything on the computer, he barely knew how to check his email. So I started up an account for him. I uploaded a photo of my father and *voila*! He was officially on Match.com.

Over the course of the next ten days, my dad went on five dates. I couldn't believe it was working. Well, actually, I could. My dad was a good-looking man at fifty-four years of age, he was six feet tall, around a hundred and seventy-five pounds—a nice build—and he still had all of his thick brown hair. Not too many guys his age could say that.

After seeing my dad go on these dates, a thought came to my head. I don't know why I didn't think of it before. *Why don't I try it too?* I was single. I thought about all the girls I had met at bars. I didn't want to settle down with any of them. I consider myself relatively charming. And a pretty good looking lad, so I should be able to find someone on Match.com—someone that would meet my list of requirements.

Without further hesitation, I signed up that weekend and decided I would find the woman of my dreams too. Why the hell not? I wasn't a spring chicken anymore and I'd had no luck with women anywhere else. I was looking for a queen I could spoil. Ultimately, I was simply looking for a person who could put up with my crap.

As soon as I signed up, I scanned over a bunch of women who looked interesting. What caught my attention the most was dark hair, tan skin and a pretty, pearly-white smile. I can admit the looks attracted me, but if the women's interests were completely different from mine, I moved on.

I was over the bar scene. I wasn't looking for somebody that wanted to get sloshed every weekend. I was looking for a woman with class and sophistication. A girl that wanted something more in this life. A girl that wanted to travel the world and it definitely had to be someone around my age.

The first one that caught my eye was a girl named La Patricia. She was one year older than I was, which I liked—I had never dated a girl older than me before. She fit the profile to a T, a nice, bright smile, dark hair and skin. She hadn't shared many interests in her profile, but it was worth a shot. Something else that caught my eye from the very get-go was her name. She had the same name as my mom. This was an added bonus. It felt like a sign to me.

I scoured over a couple dozen profiles before I wrote two more girls. I wrote the same little blurb to them as well.

La Patricia must have been online at the same time, because minutes later I received a message back from her. She said hi and introduced herself. As any clever women would, she asked two vital questions right off the bat. "What made you come to Match.com? What are your intentions?"

"I'm not here to mess around," I replied. I couldn't help but laugh. These questions were straight to the point. I answered honestly and I guess she liked what she heard, because she wrote me back immediately.

This time she asked some more specific questions. "What are your top five movies? What kind of music do you like to listen to?"

Okay, I have a ton of favorite movies and it is hard to

146

narrow it down to a top five, but I gave it my best shot. I didn't want to list all action movies or all comedy movies. I needed to mix it up a bit. I decided to throw a little curveball at her. Out of my top five, I listed *The Notebook* as one of them. Yep. The same movie that some men couldn't get through if their lives depended on it.

I am a pretty sensitive guy though and I wanted to see her reaction. I'm not a big fan of watching *chick-flicks* all the time, but I enjoy them occasionally. I have even been known to let a few tears loose if it's a really heartfelt movie. In the past, I had dated girls that hated movies like this, so if she didn't like *The Notebook*, there was a chance I wouldn't get any further. This was a little pop quiz for her in a way too. I love romance and sensitive girls. I'm a big fan of the girly-girl types. Sure, I love sports and manly stuff, but I don't want to settle down with a tomboy-type either. She was remarkably impressed with this particular selection.

February 14, 2009 my dad and I went to the breeder's house to pick up my brand-new golden retriever puppy. Dad was going to help me raise Ryder for the next few weeks while I was at school for most of the day. It was Valentine's Day and it was the first time I called Patricia on the telephone, too.

We agreed to meet up that next Thursday for dinner and drinks and decided Green Iguana would be a solid place to go. On a first date, you don't want to go anywhere too fancy so Green Iguana seemed like the perfect place to go because of its laid-back atmosphere. Plus there was a place to sit outside if we wanted. Considering it was still February, sitting outside seemed like a viable option.

It was all set. We were good to go for Thursday, February 19, 2009. A day that would live in infamy for us.

I was really tired that day, so I took a nap after school got out.

My dad came home about six thirty p.m. and knocked on my door. "Ryan, aren't you supposed to be at Green Iguana at seven o'clock?"

I looked at my alarm clock. *Shit!* "Yeah, I'm getting up right now," I answered back.

I showered and got dressed in a nice but casual outfit—a red Express polo and Express jeans. I put on my Gucci shoes for good measure. Patricia worked at Express and I knew that, so I thought it might impress her a little bit.

I'm late most of the time I go anywhere and tonight was no exception. To make it even lamer, Green Iguana is only a five-minute drive away and I still couldn't make it on time. I was a little apprehensive as I pulled into the parking lot and a whirlwind of thoughts swirled throughout my head. *What if she didn't look anything like her picture? What if she was missing her two-front teeth?* The possibilities were endless and my imagination even more so.

I looked around aimlessly. I had no clue what kind of car she had. There she was. At least I thought it was when I saw dark hair flowing in the breeze. She was on her phone standing about fifty feet away, right next to a red Hyundai Tiburon. I was almost positive it was her.

My hands started to sweat. *Dammit Ryan. Take it easy. No need to get nervous, just play it cool.* I needed to exude confidence so she thought I was cool. With every step that brought me closer, my heart seemed to beat faster. *It was her.* I was only about ten feet away.

She turned and smiled the biggest and most beautiful smile I have ever laid eyes on. *Damn, this girl is gorgeous.* She was the epitome of my perfect girl. I noticed everything about her. Her hair was beautiful and dark and her skin was flawless and sun-kissed to perfection. I couldn't help but notice she was wearing teal eye shadow. I had never really seen this color on a girl before. The jeans she was wearing fit her curves nicely and her black top looked amazing, it matched her hair perfectly.

"Hey, Patricia. I'm Ryan." I smiled what I hoped was my warmest smile. "Nice to meet you."

"Nice to meet you," she answered back. "You had me a little worried there. I didn't think you were going to show."

"I'm so sorry I'm running late. I took a nap after school and just woke up at six thirty."

"That's okay. I'm just glad you made it." She had a big smile.

We were seated outside as we'd wanted, and it was time to begin the interview. That's what a first date is, after all.

The waitress came by and took our drink order. As we began our conversation, I was instantly captivated by Patricia's energy, personality and her beauty. Being from the Midwest, I simply hadn't seen many girls like her before. She was exotic looking. At that moment, I felt like a little boy realizing he liked girls for the first time.

We talked about life, work, past relationships and past experiences. In a little over an hour, I had already realized there was something different about her. We still barely knew each other, but I could tell something special just might come out of this. I had to go to the bathroom and text my dad, "Holy shit. This girl is awesome and beautiful as well. I don't want to jinx myself before anything happens, but this girl might be the one."

Everything she said was on point with what I wanted in a woman. She thought exes were exes for a reason and

149

that it was unnecessary to remain friends. This is exactly how I felt. She believed in God, but wasn't super religious. She believed that family comes first. She told me that her parents were older; especially her dad, and at times in her life, she'd had to make sacrifices to help him and her family out. There were no spring break trips, no college parties. She'd worked a lot and some of the money that she earned went towards helping her parents pay bills and the mortgage.

She was sexy, classy and sophisticated, but what set her apart from other girls this perfect is she was so down to earth and not at all stuck up. This seemed like it could be a match made in heaven.

After dinner, we hugged and went our separate ways. I wasn't going to try to rush this. I felt like I had plenty of time to get to know her better. I jumped into my car and blasted the stereo. I felt like I was on cloud nine. I was so pumped up. What a breath of fresh air. I really did feel like a schoolboy that developed his first crush.

Chapter Twenty-Five
The Proposal

Patricia and I fell in love within just a few short weeks. I still remember saying I love you to her like it was yesterday. The school year was going smoothly. I was a much happier person being in love with Patricia. The little things didn't seem to bother me at school anymore. I'm sure I was much more pleasant to be around, and being less crabby, as a girl in class made the comment, "Mr. Krohn must have a girlfriend now."

I couldn't stop laughing, and I confided to the classroom that she was right. I didn't like to tell kids my personal business, but I was gleaming from head to toe. "Yes, matter of fact, I do have a girlfriend now."

The girls in my classroom gushed and told me how sweet it was that I finally had somebody. The boys in the classroom made inappropriate remarks as boys do. "Mr. Krohn is finally getting laid, one of them yelled."

I couldn't help but laugh at his remark. It was okay. It was the end of the year again and we were ready to be out of here.

Patricia opened me up to things I hadn't really experienced before. She is very spiritual and comes from a very spiritual family. She believes in positive energy and karma, that if you put positive energy out to the world; positive things will come into your life.

One day she asked me why I didn't have photos of my mom in my condo. That was a very good question. I don't know why I didn't have any pictures hanging up anywhere. I had a few photos of my mom and me, but they were in my dresser drawer. Patricia helped me realize in order to help keep Mom's memory alive, pictures should be scattered all over our house.

During one of our trips to Michigan, unbeknownst to me, Patricia brought down a bunch of old photos of my family, including some of my mom and me. As a surprise, she made me a photo collage from my childhood and adolescence. Most of these pictures included my mom and dad. Some of them included Taryn and Damon as well. The pictures also consisted of my high school graduation, prom, senior night in basketball and me as a newborn with my mom and dad. I hadn't seen many of these pictures in so long. It was one of the most caring things that anyone has ever done for me. I appreciated it so much.

Because of Patricia, I realized that these photos would help me remember the good times I spent with my mom and my family. Keeping the great memories alive can perpetuate a positive vibe in the house.

Summer approached and it was hotter than hell again. It was the beginning of July and our relationship was stronger than ever. I had passed the test of meeting her parents' standards. I decided it was time—time to pop the question. After I received the blessing from her father, it was time to make it happen.

I had been envisioning this night for years. I'm sure it was pretty comical, because it's a day that some men dread, not me. I had always been looking forward to the day I asked the perfect woman to be my wife.

I had purchased the most beautiful diamond ring from Tiffany's and Co. at Tampa International Mall. Thank God I had the summer off, because getting this thing was a whole job in itself. I knew that I wanted to get something spectacular. Truthfully, she would have been happy if I got her a ring out of a gumball machine, but I wanted to profess my love for her to the entire world.

The specific ring that I wanted was actually at a Tiffany's store in San Jose and they had to make some important calls to have it flown down to Tampa. I felt like a celebrity. That is the way they treat you at Tiffany's. It would take a few more days to get the ring down here from San Jose, which was perfect because it gave me a few days to plan something extra.

I knew that I wanted to write Patricia a very special poem. Also, I wanted to secure a reservation at one of the best restaurants in Tampa. After dinner, the plan was to take her to Clearwater beach and propose, standing right next to the ocean. Yes, ladies and gentlemen, your boy is a romantic that loves to please his lady.

The day had finally come. It was July 13, 2009. I had a reservation at Charley's in downtown Tampa—it is very expensive, but it is definitely one of the best places in Tampa to eat. Many people had told me that Charley's had the best steak in the entire city. Ultimately, I decided it would be the perfect place for us to go.

I was nervous that day. I noticed my hands were shaking when I brushed my teeth in preparation of going out. I hadn't been this nervous in awhile. Patricia knew we were going out to dinner at Charley's, but she didn't suspect anything out of the ordinary.

We had a fabulous dinner. The steak and fish tasted fantastic. It really did live up to the expectation of having the best food in the city. We each had a couple drinks and I told her we would be going to Clearwater Beach later that night. By the time we finished, it was nine thirty.

It was a short thirty-minute drive to Clearwater and then we parked in a parking lot near the ocean. The ring was in my trunk. I was able to open the trunk and grab it without her noticing. The night was absolutely perfect. The heat was a bit overwhelming but there was a perfect summer breeze coming from the ocean—I loved the smell of the ocean. The saltwater in the ocean had never smelled better. The scent of cooked steak and fish from the various restaurants along the road wafted through the air too.

As we walked in the sand, my nerves increased. I wanted to enjoy the moment to the fullest, but I couldn't help wanting to get it done fast just to relieve my anxiety.

Finally, I found a place by the ocean where nobody was in sight. I pulled out the poem that I had written earlier that week. I looked into Patricia's beautiful, brown eyes and began to read.

"My Love. To my beautiful Patricia, the love of my life.

I can't wait until the day I call you wife.

The first moment we met, I knew something was there.

I was enticed by the gorgeous smile, dark skin and dark hair.

Sweet romance blossomed that very first date.

Sent from heaven above, it must have been fate.

One of the happiest times ever was that first kiss.

The touching of our lips and hands was eternal bliss.

"Our love started off quick and grew stronger and stronger.

Every time we are together, I yearn for you longer.

Living together, my happiest dreams have come true.

It's impossible to love somebody more than I love you.

I promise to love you and our families all my life.

I can't wait to be called husband and to call you my wife"

I finished reading and got down on bended knee. "I am totally and completely enamored with you, Patricia. I love you more than anything in the world. I love you more than life itself. I have been waiting for this moment for a long, long time."

She started to freak out. "Oh my God, this is it!"

"Patricia, will you marry me?"

"Yes, of course I will!" She wore the biggest smile I'd ever seen and she had tears in her eyes.

We kissed and hugged each other for what seemed like a lifetime. Then we called and texted everybody we knew. We stayed up until two a.m. just talking with people about our new life together. We couldn't possibly have been happier. We had both been looking forward to this our whole lives.

Chapter Twenty-Six
The Wedding

It was time for one of the most magical times of our lives. Patricia and I were getting married on March 20, 2010. We had hired a wedding planner to help us and it was the busiest time in our lives. We were both working like crazy and trying to plan this wedding. Patricia did almost of all the work with our wedding planner. Matter of fact, Patricia did such a fantastic job, I told her that she could be a wedding planner herself and do as good a job as anyone.

School was going pretty well. I had my ups and downs like everybody, but overall the good outweighed the bad. My junior varsity basketball team finished with a promising 11-5 record. We beat the best team in the district on a buzzer beater, which made me so proud.

We had invited approximately eighty-five people to the wedding. Not too big. Not too small. Prior to the wedding and deciding on what we wanted to do, we had almost decided to elope to an island somewhere. We both decided against it because we wanted our families to take part in this joyous occasion with us.

I was happy because my best friends and family would all be flying down from Michigan. Even my best friend, Sam, would be one of the groomsmen. We liked to tease him because he had never really been anywhere. The furthest south he had ever been was Fort Wayne, Indiana. He joked and said his head would probably explode the moment they drove into Kentucky.

We were getting married on Siesta Key Beach in Sarasota. Siesta Key is by far one of the most beautiful beaches in the whole United States. It is perennially ranked in the top ten for best beaches in the whole country. Matter of fact, Dr. Beach—the so-called expert of beaches—ranked it at number two for 2010. It was actually ranked number one last year in 2011. It is widely recognized as having the whitest and finest sand anywhere.

Needless to say, the location of our wedding ceremony would be exquisite. The weather was typically perfect at this time of year. However, this year was a little different. The winter had been colder than in years past, so I was little worried it would rain or be on the chilly side.

When our wedding planner initially set up March 20 as the date months before, she had assured us it wouldn't rain. Obviously she isn't God, and she can't predict the future, but luckily she ended up being right. The entire months of March and April are usually perfect and we expected it to be in the upper 70's, sunny and clear, with only a few clouds in the sky, if any. Well, it didn't seem like we were going to get that. It had been chilly the last few days plus the rain had been sporadic. It was hit or miss.

It was now March 19, 2010. One day before the big day. The weather was chilly that day. We were hoping for a warmer day on the twentieth—I wanted it to be beautiful.

I woke up nervous on the twentieth, but when I got up to look outside it was sunny. "Hopefully it lasts," I said to Damon. The forecast looked promising. Mid seventies and only a ten percent chance of rain.

I already had butterflies in my stomach. I needed to eat something. Damon and Cole, my brother-in-law, brought me a bagel and a coffee. It was the worst tasting coffee I have ever had, but I didn't care. I needed some caffeine to wake me up and help me focus. I was a little hung-over from the night before.

Surrounded by eighty-five of our best friends and family, we put a label on the love we'd felt for each other from the first moment of our fourth date. I can still see the huge smile on Patricia's face, her caramel skin glistening in the sunshine, and her body wrapped in the most glorious dress I had ever seen. Her make-up and hair were worth the hours it took to prepare. She really was a princess. Her beauty commanded the attention of everyone at the ceremony, and not simply because she was the bride. Her presence and charisma attracted everybody. I can still remember the scent of Hanae Mori permeating in the air.

The reception took place down the road just a few miles. It was beautiful and set off in the woods. Yes, we got married on a beach and then celebrated at a cathedral in the wilderness. I thought that was amazing. The photographers took a ton of stunning photos of us. We were ready for the next chapter of our lives.

Chapter Twenty-Seven
Gifts From Beyond

I was settling into married life nicely. Patricia and I were definitely happy newlyweds. We took a mini-honeymoon to Sanibel Island and stayed at my aunt and uncle's house. We enjoyed spending our time in the pool by day and the Jacuzzi at night. It's a fabulous house and a perfect place to relax.

We decided that we wanted to go to Riviera Maya for our real honeymoon. We had to postpone it though because of work. We also decided not to go to Mexico in the summer because Florida is hot enough. We would go in the winter of 2011. At least then it would feel like we were actually taking advantage of a tropical location.

In the summertime of 2010, we got the chance we to go to Michigan for a couple weeks. We stayed at my dad's house in Portage. Taryn lived close by and Chicago was only a couple hours away. It doesn't get any better than Chicago in the summer time. Damon and Anjie lived in Chicago and they loved to show us around the city.

While in Michigan, I needed to do something very important. I needed to drive down to Jonesville—for a few different reasons. First, to see my grandma and aunt because living twelve hundred miles away didn't give me the opportunity to see them on a regular basis. I only got up there once a year. I thought I should get up there more often. Mom would have liked me to get up there as much as I can.

Patricia had never been to Jonesville. We borrowed one of my dad's five cars and decided to trek it down to Jonesville. I was excited to make the drive with her. Patricia had heard many stories of Jonesville and where I grew up, yet hadn't had the privilege to visiting until this day.

We headed south down I-69 and I saw a familiar sign Exit Number 16-Jonesville Road Exit. From there we had about twenty more minutes until we reached Jonesville.

Patricia was amazed at all the farmland and vegetation. I couldn't blame her. We didn't have this in Florida—at least not in our area. We were driving down Jonesville road passing farm after farm. "I feel like we're in the movie *Field of Dreams*," she said, laughing.

"You're right," I said. "That is kind of what it's like around here. Kind of feels like we're in the middle of nowhere. But there are no ghosts here like in the movie. At least none that I know of."

"What is that?" Patricia asked with excitement. My car came to a screeching halt. Patricia's reaction was priceless. I was expecting to see an alien or something by the way her voice sounded.

"Oh wow." I laughed. "It's an Amish buggy. I can't say I've seen one of these in awhile."

"Wait...what?" Patricia had a look of shock on her face. "An Amish buggy? I thought these people didn't exist anymore."

As I sat there dying from laughter, I almost flew off the road. When we passed the Amish buggy, I made sure to drive by nice and slow. "Looks like we're stuck in the eighteenth century, eh?"

There were three boys and a girl in the buggy. The boys had beards and were dressed like something you thought you would only see in the movies.

160

"Wow that is crazy," she said. "I thought I was in a movie for a minute."

And this is why I love Patricia so much—it's moments like these that I'll never forget. Patricia cracks me up in a way I thought a woman never could. Not only is she my beautiful wife, but she is the funniest person ever.

We made the turn onto Highway 12. A road so familiar, but so unfamiliar at the same time. "Here we are," I said with a huge smile on my face. "This is Jonesville. This is where it all began."

Patricia was excited for me. In the few years that I'd lived in Florida, I hadn't been back much. When I did come back, it was usually to Kalamazoo and Portage. I didn't make the trip to Jonesville very often. To be quite honest, a part of me missed it, but at the same time a large part of me realized why I didn't come here very often.

It wasn't that I didn't love the place where I grew up—I love seeing my family and the people who I grew up with, we will always share a common bond—but something happened here that is still so heavily engraved in my brain that it has scarred me for life. I remember so vividly what this place did to me. What it did to our family. And most important, what it did to my mom. I don't blame Jonesville for Mom's death, but this is where it happened. This is where so much pain and agony lives within my heart.

There was no escaping it. I had to go through the intersection where the accident happened. It was the only way so I could get to the cemetery where my mom rests— the only way I could show Patricia Jonesville High School.

As we glided through the intersection, all the thoughts and emotions came back, all rolled into one. I remember the maelstrom and I remember what happened that fateful evening. I started to tear up as Patricia rubbed the back of my neck. I have never been so happy and bitter at the same time.

"Let's go to the cemetery first," I told her.

"We need to stop somewhere first, Ryan," she said.

Where could we need to stop? I was confused. She doesn't know this area.

Patricia looked me in the eyes and chimed back in. "We need to go to a flower shop and get your mom some flowers. Your mother's site deserves flowers, and we're going to make sure she has some."

She was right. People visit her site and I'm sure they drop off flowers, but I needed to also. This was another reason my wife is so special to me—because I was sad, I didn't even think of it, but my wife always puts my needs first. I'm so lucky to have her.

We pulled up to my mom's gravesite and there it was. Something I've only visited a handful of times. I see Krohn on the back of the head stone.

Patricia and I got out of the car and walked to see my mom. Although, she wasn't there with us, I would like to think and believe that my wife was meeting my mother for the first time.

Flowers in hand, I turned to the tombstone and spoke. "Hi, Mom, it's Ryan. Sorry it's been awhile. I wanted to introduce you to my wife, Patricia. Yes, she has the same name as you. I know that you already knew that because you have been looking down on us. How cool is it that she has the same name as you? She is so beautiful, Mom. And she treats me like a king. You would love her."

Patricia was crying and it made me tear up a little more. "I just wanted to say hello and that I love you—we love you. Everything is going great down in Florida. All the kids are doing great. Damon is graduating with his master's from Northwestern. He is going for his PhD in counseling. Taryn is doing great with Cole. She is working at a hotel downtown and loving life. Dad is doing fine. He is finally happy and at peace with everything, I think. He misses you so much though. We all do."

My tears were flowing like crazy, as they soaked my hand and the stems of the red tulips I was holding. "I know that you're proud of us. You'll always be a part of me and I'll always be a part of you. I love you. I will see you again one day."

After a few minutes of just looking down in silence, I told Patricia that I wanted to see the rest of my family members. My Grandpa Langs was here. My Uncle Jerry rests here along with my two cousins—Jared and Jaime. They were both around my age and had both passed away in the last few years as well. I went over to see my former high school basketball coach. Coach Dunn had made a strong impact in my life as well. A few feet away from there, lay Dustin Hale. I never knew him, but he was the son of my favorite teacher, Judy Hale.

Before we left, I went back over to my mom's site for a couple more minutes. I took comfort in knowing that my family were all together. They were looking down on us from a place that is much better than here.

"There is just one more stop I need to make before we go see my Grandma and aunt," I said. "I want to go see our house on Walnut Street."

"Whatever you want to do, baby," Patricia said. "This is your day."

We left the cemetery and I had a smile on my face. I felt better after seeing my mom. In my heart and soul, I knew that she was watching down on us. I can't really explain it. Just various things have happened over the years that make me believe so. Patricia and I pulled up to 137 Walnut St. *There it is.* The old blue ranch house in which I grew up. The house wasn't too big and it wasn't too small. It included a basketball hoop, a large backyard, and a pool in the back.

I knocked on the door and introduced myself to the people that lived there. The place looked different on the inside. I guess they had done some remodeling.

The guy welcomed me with open arms and we talked for a few minutes. "Come to think of it, there is a box in our garage that I think belongs to you guys," he said. "I found it when we first moved in."

"Okay thanks," I said, "I'll check it out."

We all walked into my old garage and he gave me a little box. I looked inside of it. There were a few old pictures of my family, a couple baseballs and piece of paper.

"What is this?" I said aloud to Patricia.

I opened up the paper and it was the note my dad wrote right after my mom passed away. My dad was so strong in the few days after my mom's passing. He wrote a beautiful letter to her, addressing his undying love for her. In the paragraphs, he described the first time they met and a very specific day when we all went to Binder Park Zoo.

It was a very touching letter. My dad's nickname for my mom was Irishred. He wrote the letter himself, but it was supposed to be from all of us. I looked at the title last. The title of the letter said, *Our Beloved Red.*

I knew I wanted to keep the letter and the photos. I gave the guy the box and the baseballs. I thanked him and then Patricia and I got in my dad's car. It was time to go see the rest of my family.

THE END

Acknowledgments

Any omissions are unintentional.

Without the help of the following people, this book would not be possible: Mom, Dad, Taryn, Damon, and Patricia.

A very special thanks to all the families that were there for us during this time of need: the Sheerer family, the Langs family, the White family, the Molinaro family, the Lessard family, and the whole community of Jonesville which consists of too many people to list. You guys are all very much appreciated.

Extra special thanks to my editor Lisa Dawn Martinez, my cover artist Kim Vanmeter, and my formatter/designer, Judi Fennell.

Author's Bio

Growing up in small-town Michigan, Ryan Krohn played a ton of sports as he was quite the athlete. However, for practically 3-4 months out of the year, it was too cold and snowy to play anything outside. When he wasn't in school, he was reading and writing little short stories of his very own. His parents stated that he was very creative and inquisitive from an early age. His beloved mother stated that he got bored with toys and video games so he would write and just make up stories for fun.

In high school and college he loved to write as well, but never took it that serious. He wrote poems, song lyrics, and lyrics for rap songs as well. He even won a couple awards in his college writing courses at Western Michigan University.

After his mother passed away in a tragic car accident, he used writing as a tool to help him deal with feelings of sadness and loneliness.

Ryan Krohn resides in Florida with his beautiful wife and two pets. He is currently writing another memoir on the loss of his uncle and two cousins. Dive into his blog at http://ourbelovedred.blogspot.com/ to see his latest blog posts about life, love, and loss as we know it.